Romantic Texas

Love in its essence is spiritual fire.
~ Emanuel Swedenborg

ROMANTIC TEXAS and the ROMANTIC AMERICA series
are published and produced by
KC Designs
4178 Sorrento Valley Blvd. ♥ Suite I
San Diego, California 92121
Copyright 1996
All rights reserved.

Designed & Formatted By:

fsquare
Creative Services Group
San Diego, California
fsquare@inetworld.net • http://www.inetworld.net/~pdqshop/fsquare.htm
619.740.1131

Cover Photos:
Sailboats & Sunrise: Robert Fletcher
Linden Lake: Pat Calloway

No portions of this book may be reproduced -- mechanically, electronically or by any other means including photocopying, recording or information storage or retrieval systems -- without permission in writing from the publisher/author.

The contents of this book are based on the best available information and references at the time of research. The publisher/author assumes no liability arising from the publishing of material in this book or of actions of advertisers or readers of this book. Does anybody ever really read this part? *"Hi mom!"*

Dedicated to those who practice, strive for, unselfishly share, and who will always believe in...

The Art of Romance

♥ ♥

♥ ♥

Traveling The Romantic Highway

The Romantic Highways of Texas lead you through portions of the state with easy access in and around metropolitan areas. Using North East Texas as a starting point, we gradually travel south until we reach South Padre Island.

With the eminence of the 21st century looming precariously overhead, and the fastest pace life-styles ever in the history of mankind, more and more couples want to "Take a Break" or "Getaway" from the rest of the world, even if only for a day, week or weekend. *Romantic Texas* is designed just for those people and serves as an inspiration to those searching for unusual things to do.

Join me on a journey through a state so surprisingly diverse in scenery and dazzling beauty that you are sure to delight in all of the areas listed in this book. Enjoy!

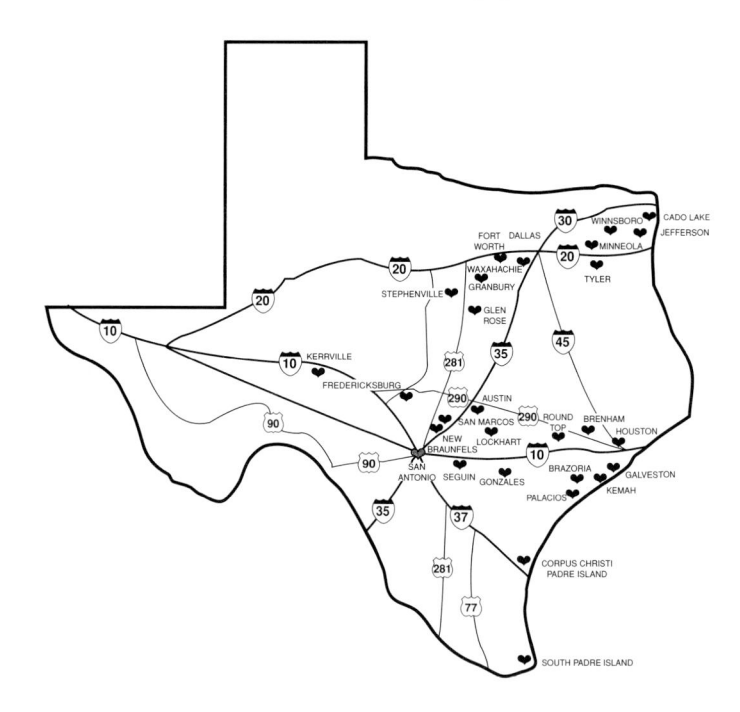

Table of Contents

North East Texas & Piney Woods 11

North Central Texas 29

Austin 47

The Texas Hill County 59

San Antonio 83

Wildflower Country 95

Houston 109

Out And About The Gulf Coast 117

Recipes For Romance 133

The Art Of Romance

by Michelle-Paige Malone

Romance means many things to many people. The true "Art of Romance", for romance *is* an art, can flourish at different levels and stages of a relationship if you pay attention to your partner's individual likes and dislikes.

The art of being romantic, even seductive, involves personal creativity. This book can help with suggestions but *you have to do the research*. Refining your instincts about the "Art of Romance" requires work and imagination. Once understood and mastered, you can enjoy the ever-ongoing satisfaction of a successful relationship.

One of the key factors of romanticism is the ability to establish your own style, a style that becomes second nature once you become comfortable with it. This gives you a personalized signature, a "gift" that is lovingly bestowed upon any new or continuing relationship.

Your own style of romance is a special quality which sets you apart from the crowd -- a quality that can bring pleasure and joy into your life and that of others. Believe me, it's worth the time, effort and love you put into any relationship.

Is It Really Romantic?

Romance can be subtle or taken to extremes. The choice is yours. What may work for one person or a couple may not work for others. Look for happy mediums (rather than compromising), without overdoing it, especially while getting to know someone. Experiment, be open, and find your own limits.

I encourage couples to recognize and savor a comfortable mood or atmosphere while establishing a relationship. Keep things low-key, without expectations, and you will get the chance to know someone better, even if you've been together for some time.

Because I believe that everyone is destined in life to experience *True Love*, if no one is in your life at this particular moment, don't fret. Keep an eye open for potentially good experiences. Then, when you do find that special someone, you will be ready (if you've done your homework).

CHILDREN AND ROMANTIC GETAWAYS

Although children are allowed at some B&Bs and most hotels, keep in mind that the purpose of your visit is to enhance your relationship and give you the chance to be alone together. Just about every couple knows someone who won't mind taking care of their children for a day or two, especially if you explain to them the desire of spending quality time together alone.

IN SEARCH OF THE ULTIMATE BUBBLE BATH

Just about all of the lodgings in this publication have comfortable bathrooms and spacious bathtubs. A very romantic evening can be centered around a shared bubble bath allowing the opportunity to relax and have fun together. Bring some bubbles (a little shampoo works great if not supplied), candles and champagne for an intimate, sensual experience worth remembering.

DRINKING: ON A PERSONAL NOTE

When referring to drinking, one should not necessarily assume it is an alcoholic beverage. In changing times when numerous people consume little or no alcoholic beverages, or for that matter, may not be of proper age, there are a number of substitutes available to please the palate. Non alcoholic champagne and wines are also available.

Sparkling Cider, fruit juice, plain or flavoured mineral waters are readily available in grocery stores. Coffee, tea, Cappuccino and Espresso as well as the aforementioned drinks are good liquor replacements in just about any restaurants. P.S.: A mixture of champagne and orange juice (Mimosa) can also go a long way.

ROMANTIC AMERICA'S GUARANTEE TO OUR READERS:

All of the restaurants, lodgings and experiences in this book have been researched extensively and have been visited personally by the authors. Although there is a reasonable participation charge in order to cover publishing expenses, the authors are extremely selective about who appears in the Romantic America series. Hence, you can be sure of a pleasurable experience whenever you visit businesses listed in this book.

Bed & Breakfast Inns

Bed and Breakfast Inns are a delightful way to spend a day, weekend or week when an escape from everyday life is desperately needed. Honeymoons, anniversaries and special events are the perfect avenues for using B&Bs as an excuse to enjoy life to the fullest. Proprietors at these establishments assure that you are comfortable and relaxed, so enjoy the extra attention.

Many people believe that all B&B's are decorated in a Victorian motif and have shared baths. Not always so! All of the lodgings in this book offer a wide variety of decor and styles that will please even the most critical traveller. Very few B&B's have a shared bath, and on the average, have private bathroom with a charming decor. An excellent place to begin a romantic adventure!

Because B&B's are not always everyone's cup of tea, considerable emphasis has been put on Inns and Hotels also. Some prefer the extra amenities a fine hotel can provide, while others prefer not to save money by using a reasonably lesser priced inn/hotel. This way, travel monies can focus on dining experiences and local attractions and your escape need not be a burden to your pocketbook. So have no fear...you don't have to have a lot of money to have a great time!

Guestroom rates are listed at the end of every review. Keep in mind that many smaller establishments have off-season rates that will fit many limited budgets.

Romantic Dining

Here is a secret to enjoying a truly romantic and relaxing dinner: Make reservations for 7:30 or 8:00. This gives you plenty of time to get ready without rushing from work or your lodging where you now have the opportunity to enjoy a glass of champagne or sparkling cider in the comfort of your surroundings. Once you are seated for dinner, order a cocktail and appetizer. By the time your main course arrives, you'll find that a good percentage of the restaurant has cleared out, allowing the opportunity to enjoy and savour the rest of your evening in a quiet and subdued atmosphere.

Historic Accommodations of Texas

Historic Accommodations of Texas is an association of Texas' finest bed and breakfasts, country inns, hotels and guesthouses, each with significant ties to Texas history.

With over 100 members in all corners of the state, from beaches to Piney Woods, to rivers and ranch country, HAT is the travelling public's assurance that the inn they select can measure up to high expectations. With over 800 inns in Texas now, and travelers' leisure time increasingly valuable, making the correct choice can be a challenge. This is where HAT can help.

The organization is highly selective, accepting only the most beautiful and significant properties in any given region. Not only do applicants have to be recognized historic treasures, they must be impeccably maintained and professionally run. Once accepted, members participate in regular inspection visits and educational programs.

The end result is that whether your heart's desire is a farmhouse in the bluebonnets, a romantic Victorian mansion, or a sophisticated boutique hotel, look first for that coveted HAT logo. If you find it, you can be sure you have found one of the best lodgings in Texas.

For a free brochure, call 800.HAT.8669

Love Note...

If you are searching for a quiet and romantic experience, you may want to consider working on the weekends and then taking a couple of weekdays off. Many lodging establishments are not very busy during the week at this time and you will be surprised to find that a larger selection of rooms are available to choose from. In fact, you just may have the whole house to yourself!

Romantic Texas?

In my many travels throughout the United States, Texas was always a mystery. While on driving excursions from Chicago to the ski slopes of Colorado in my youth, my vision of Texas was the desert of the Panhandle. In fact, many people who have travelled this route have a similar vision of this vast state. Inspired by the Beach Boys song Surfin U.S.A. "Two girls for every boy" (one of the biggest lies of the century), I moved to California and thought I had discovered paradise. Upon further exploration of Texas in Spring 1996, this perspective has changed considerably!

Surprisingly, when I told people that I was researching this book, the general response was..."What's Romantic about Texas"? My reply was always... "A lot!"

Diversified landscapes including the Northeast Piney Woods, the beautiful Hill Country and vast stretches of open beach in the coastal areas, never cease to amaze. Friendly residents go out of there way to share the famous, "Texas Hospitality" and a statewide camaraderie is nothing short of charming. Searching for the Texas Star incorporated in just about anything and everything was also a fun experience.

Little quirks that I didn't think much about at first, became increasingly apparent during my travels, especially in the rural areas and small towns. Here are some favourites; Wal-Mart, frequently referred to as Wally World, was almost revered, every town had a Dairy Queen, people say "Hey" instead of Hello, and when you asked for directions, it was consistently "Turn at the red light", never the green light. No sissy water fountains in this state! Stand back because the average stream of water is 8"+.

What this all boils down to, is that... "By golly, I really liked Texas!"

An endless list of unique excursions made it challenging to keep this book to a reasonable size. However, for those in search of romantic outlets, you are sure to find many wonderful, and affordable, ideas in this publication. Throughout this book there is an assortment of information guaranteed to keep the spark alive in any relationship.

So sit back and enjoy Romantic Texas. You now have that long awaited opportunity to share unforgettable adventures with your significant other!

North East Texas and Piney Woods

*Nothing is sweeter than love
Nothing stronger,
Nothing loftier
Nothing fuller,
Nothing better in heaven or on earth.*

~ Henri Matisse

What a great way to discover Texas! Here, the four-seasons paint beautiful landscapes and delight the senses all year-round. Scenic highways lead to many lakes dotting the countryside and serve as a destination for a "Sunday Drive and Picnic". Hundreds of towns, each with its own special history have a variety of arts and crafts, antiques, unique stores, restaurants, historical museums and homes. The town of Canton is a great antiquing destination at the First Monday Trade Days on the weekend before the first Monday of each month.

The Northeast Texas Tourism Council has a colourful map that displays all of the towns in a 75 mile radius and features 22 "Cities to Visit". This is a handy travel guide to have when visiting this area and can be had by calling any of Chamber of Commerce listed in this chapter.

Enjoy! I did!

Getting Away From It All

*T*here are times when a romantic getaway, far from the city, is an absolute must! So with this book in hand, pack your bags, hop in your car, and discover many small towns, less than a two hour drive away. All offer their own brand of individual Southern Hospitality and many have a quaint Bed & Breakfast Inn.

*N*ortheast Texas is exceptionally beautiful and has many rural roads that take you through endless forests of towering pines. For a great romantic excursion, choose any of the destination points listed in these chapters and plot out a journey that takes you into the heart of two or three towns. The average speed on the open road is 65 ~ 70 m.p.h. which gradually reduces to 25 m.p.h. until you reach the city limits.

*M*ost of these towns have a courthouse or town hall, (many were built in the first half of this century) each has a unique construction style. This is a great opportunity to park your car and explore the area in search of a restaurant, soda shop or antique store. Be sure to bring a camera and start a collection of Texas architecture.

Antiquing ~ Always a fun excursion, especially when getting to know someone. Most of the towns listed in this book have an assortment of antique shops worth exploring. Searching out unique treasures can be a truly unforgettable adventure. Some towns have charity outlet stores where you can go Junkin', and you may be surprised at what you find! Make a game of your excursion by starting in the morning in search of something that costs $1.00 or less. Then, have a fine lunch and spend the afternoon seeking out an expensive treasure.

In Search Of The Antiqualope ~ As you become increasingly familiar with the fine art of antiquing, you may discover a curious form of creature called an Antiqualope. Exhibiting a peculiar type of behavior patterns, they migrate throughout the countryside in search of the best buys around. You may overhear them saying things like; *"I'm looking for a bung hole drill and a Chippendale, I have to have a steamer trunk to hold my junk, or, AAAAAaaaaghhhh! I can't take it anymore! There's too much stuff! How can a person decide? I'm loooosing my mind!*

(Special thanks to Christopher K. Travis editor of the Round Top Gazette in Round Top, Texas, for his discovery, and, research of the Antiqualope.)

Tyler

Known as the Rose Capitol of the Nation, Tyler produces one fifth of all commercial rose bushes in the United States. Home to the Tyler Municipal Rose Garden, (the nations largest) from early May until frost, visitors can delight in over 30,000 bushes exhibiting over 400 varieties of roses. The Rose Garden Center has a gift shop and the Tyler Rose Museum has a variety of interactive exhibits that include a Parade Room with floats, hand-sewn, jeweled gowns, worn by former Rose Queens and the Attic of Memories that features antiques and collectibles from the city's past. In mid-October, the Rose Garden is the site of the annual, four-day Texas Rose Festival. Check out the popular Queen's Tea which is literally a city-wide garden party for the public. ♥ 903.597.3130 ~ Admission fee required.

Mineola

Located approximately 70 miles from Dallas and 80 miles from Shreveport, Mineola is designated as a Texas Main Street City and Lone Star City. The historic downtown district is occupied with many antique shops, specialty shops, crafts malls, four B&Bs and an artisan gallery. Year-round festivals include the May Day Fest, Railroad Heritage Days and the Yuletide Festival which begins the Saturday after Thanksgiving.

An afternoon can be spent discovering downtown and the many refurbished hotels and historic homes in the area. Stop for lunch at Kitchen's Hardware and Deli and sample New Orleans po'boys and other delights available from the old fashioned deli; then have a swig of Sarsaparilla! Browse along vintage inventory in search of a gift for your loved-one.

The historic architecture of the 70 year-old Select Theater offers first run movies, and the 1918 Lake Country Playhouse, (still in operation) was remodeled in 1948 with an Art Deco theme. If you are seeking a different kind of adventure, historic Wisener Field Airport combines history and aviation interests and has several immaculately restored biplanes and other classics.

Relax, slow down and enjoy Mineola, this is a nice break from the hustle and bustle of the big city. ♥ Mineola Chamber of Commerce: 903.569.2087 ~ 800.MIN.EOLA

Texas Eagle Train Line Comes to Mineola (well... maybe)

The Texas Eagle came into Mineola on April 29, 1996. On board were 500 East Texans celebrating the newest Texas Eagle stop since 1983. With visions of increased tourism stimulating the local economy, a crowd of 1500 townspeople rolled out the red carpet.

Less than four months later, AMTRAK is attempting to eliminate this three-times-weekly stop, blaming it on a decline of federal funding and financial loss. The citizens of Mineola are not taking this lying down and have the support of over 15 representatives and two senators. Lets see what happens! Until then, taking the train from Dallas or Longview is a great excuse to make Mineola a destination point. Newsflash: The route has been extended through May 1997!

Winnsboro

Recognized as the Christmas tree capitol of the world, visitors travel from miles around in the winter to choose the perfect tree from one of several Christmas Tree Farms in the area. A Santa Claus parade is sure to put you in the Christmas spirit.

Fine restaurants, antique shops, mini-malls B&Bs and quaint specialty shops dot the countryside and many yearly festivals, including the Spring Trial Rides and a Fourth of July celebration, are set among the dogwood trees and wildflowers. Savour the breathtaking beauty of the fall colours during the Autumn Days festival were you will be able to enjoy ten thousand horsemen, a barn dance, hundreds of antique cars and tours of many historical homes in the area.

♥ Winnsboro Chamber of Commerce 903.342.3666 ♥

Love Note...

After your dishwasher has cleaned the dishes, put a note in one of the glasses that tells your partner you will put the dishes away. This is sure to bring a smile to their face!

Charnwood Hill Inn

This opulent three story house is five star all the way. With 10,000 square feet of living space, all guest rooms and suites are extremely plush and all have their own private baths. Huge porches and columns surround three sides of the estate and a beautiful Azalea garden with lighted arbor make up the west yard. Large common areas such as the library, music room, and the quaint garden room are enjoyed by all.

Built in 1855, this property has been the home of several prominent Texans. Of these, the most well known, the late oil baron, H.L. who Hunt purchased Charnwood estate in the 1930s and from here, oversaw his now infamous oil empire. Completely renovated in 1978, this impressive home is situated on a large estate with towering trees and a large grassy yard perfect for a Southern picnic.

Guests of Charnwood enjoy wonderful antique shopping in Tyler, fantastic golf courses, beautiful lakes and parks and an abundance of fine dining and shopping. Charnwood is the perfect place for a romantic wedding and reception, or corporate functions.

CHARNWOOD INN
Guestroom rates: $95.00 – $175.00
223 East Charnwood • Tyler, Texas 75701 • 903.597.3980

STARGAZING

Its easy to see why Texas's crystal clear country skies have turned stargazing into a popular pastime. Pick an evening to take a drive away from the distraction of city lights and look for a quiet spot to pull off the road. (Plan ahead: A couple of lawn chairs, a bottle of champagne and two glasses would come in handy about now). Breathe in the cool night air, pick out the Little and Big Dippers, watch for falling stars, make outrageous wishes and savour the moment. There are many campfire spots along the lakes and rivers in Texas and it is not uncommon to see a romantic couple cozying up to the warmth of a bonfire under the starry skies.

Munzesheimer Manor

An alluring, spacious home built at the turn-of the century by Gustav Munzesheimer, the architecture is "Princess Anne" style and reflects an era of days gone by. Your hosts, Sherry and Bob Murray take great pride in welcoming you to this pleasant B&B in the heart of Mineola. Wraparound porches on three sides of the house are complete with rockers, setting the pace for a relaxing visit.

Painstakingly restored to its original splendor, this Inn has been thoroughly modernized while maintaining the charm and warmth of yesteryear. For your comfort, there is central heating and air conditioning and you will find ceiling fans in each room. Original photographs of Julia Munzesheimer, (wife of Gustav) enhance the decor.

Two parlors, a large formal dining room, and four guestrooms are in the main house. All are furnished with English and American antiques, and each has its own private bath with a claw foot tub (bubbles & rubber ducky provided). Victorian gowns and nightshirts are available for each guest, allowing the opportunity to truly take a step back in time.

Sherry is the decorator, and she has incorporated her special touch that individualizes the historical significance of each room. These rooms are named after four previous owners and three have fireplaces including the *Blasinghame Room* with a queen-sized brass bed, and *Dr. Cowans' Room*, which has a fully draped oak bed, and a dentist chair. The *Perry Room* honors the family who added electricity and plumbing in 1912. The *Thomas Room* reflects the owners ties to the publishing world, as owner of the local newspaper; The Mineola Monitor.

In the back of the property, tucked away among beautiful trees and hedges are three cottage rooms with an elegant, rustic touch. They include the *Engineer's Room* with black iron decor and a full feather bed, and the *Conductors Room*, which is like being in a railroad station. This room comes complete with a conductor's hat. The *Tack Room* in a seperate cottage, completes the offerings. It was constructed of materials from a demolished 1850s house. Guided by a letter written by a former occupant of the Manor, a two-holer was built into the bathroom.

Cute patios and porches encourage restful afternoons and evenings shared in pleasant conversation. In the early evening, enjoy a glass of sparkling cider in the cozy gazebo surrounded by manicured gardens.

A full breakfast is served family-style and may include favorites such as German pancakes with a special "Moonshine Syrup" from Louisiana and Blueberry Soup made with locally grown blueberries.

Available for special occasions such as weddings, receptions, showers, luncheons, teas, honeymoons, surprise birthdays and anniversaries, or just a romantic getaway, Munzesheimer Manor is a sparkling gem in the heart of North East Texas.

MUNZESHEIMER MANOR
Guestroom rates: $75.00 ~ $95.00 • Limited Handicap accessible
202 N. Newsom • Mineola, Texas 75773
903.569.6634

Love Note...

A SECRET FORMULA OF LOVE

First, you have to be in love with the person you marry. Keep the lines of communication open and do things together, even if it's the dishes. Go away for a weekend together. If you have a tight budget, a suburban motel is fine if that is all you can afford, surroundings aren't always important, especially if you need to "get-a-way". You would be surprised what a little tenderness and kissing can do to get you in the mood. The important thing is that you are spending quality time together.

Thee Hubbell House

*E*xquisitely situated on a tree-lined street with spacious lots and beautiful turn-of-the-century homes, this five bedroom 1888 Colonial Mansion on a two acre landscaped estate inspires visions of a gentler time and place. Porch swings and rocking chairs on the upstairs and downstairs verandas paint the perfect picture of a tranquil Southern life-style.

This Bed and Breakfast is owned and operated by Dan and Laurel Hubbell, who by their own, (and families') admission, love to play house! Dan is a former pastor, mayor and municipal judge, Laurel is a teacher near retirement, both are knowledgable resources on the history of this magical property that was meticulously restored in 1987.

There are five guestrooms with private baths in the main mansion and six rooms in the two story Carriage House. All have been authentically restored by Dan and eloquently decorated by Laurel. The spacious *Master Suite* has a four poster canopy bed and a romantic setting, the *Magnolia Room* with head board and canopy bed is a complete suite, with individual sitting and bed rooms. Both of these suites can be an inspiration for a romantic, private candlelight dinner. Fresh flowers, armoires, reading sofas and many other personal touches, add a bit of magic to all the bedrooms.

The enclosed second floor gallery porch in the Carriage House overlooks an expansive garden area with wrought iron chairs elegantly positioned around towering shade trees complete with chirping birds and wandering squirrels. This porch is an ideal spot for an afternoon nap in a comfortable chair.

There is a private sauna on this estate, the enclosed spa in the backyard can be reserved in advance and an in-house professional massage is available. An on-property antique shop in the cottage (which also has two rentable rooms) may inspire an afternoon of antiquing in town. Fruit and non-alcoholic wine is available in the parlor in the afternoon, and in the morning, a gourmet breakfast is served in the formal dining area and can include baked apples, eggs, sausage, grits, English muffins, cinnamon rolls, coffee and juice.

Weddings and tent weddings are a specialty of this property and offer easy access to wonderful honeymoon rooms. Looking for an unforgettable rendezvous? Upon request, a seven-course meal can be served by a tuxedoed staff in the privacy of your room or in the main dining area.

While visiting Thee Hubbell House, enjoy a romantic picnic in the back yard, take an afternoon drive and discover the many lakes in the area, play golf on one of many courses, or treat yourself to a walking tour of the neighborhood. A magical oasis that cradles you in comfort, peace and massive doses of Southern hospitality, Thee Hubbell House is a historic treasure you won't easily forget.

THEE HUBBELL HOUSE
Guestroom rates: $65.00 ~ $150.00
One handicapped accessible room
307 West Elm • Winnsboro, Texas 75754
903.342.5629 ~ 800.227.0639 ~ Fax: 903.342.6627

Romantic Texas · 19

Pittsburg

Another Main Street City, Pittsburg is surrounded by fields, forests and lakes that are nestled among pristine forests. Nationally known as the home of Pittsburg Hotlinks and Pilgrim's Pride Corporation, this town is deeply rooted in East Texas history. In the springtime, you can pick blueberries and blackberries from local farms or buy them roadside. The Independence Blast and Peachberry is a July 4th celebration where you can sample Camp County peaches, the best in Texas!

The historic downtown has a mix of antique shops, fashion clothing stores and restaurants. A quaint bakery is a nice break for lunch and there is a fifties soda fountain and an old-time hardware store; two great destination points. The finest restaurant in East Texas; The Carson House and Grille, is just two blocks north of downtown. Enjoy a walking tour of the area to discover historic museums, churches, homes and buildings – many built in the 1800's. Don't miss the full scale replica of the 1902 Ezekiel Airship at Warrick's Restaurant. This was built by Rev. Cannon and actually flew over Pittsburg a full year before the Wright brothers took flight!

As you stroll though downtown in the early evening, the beautiful chimes from the bell tower and chapel at Witness Park, inspire soothing thoughts of what rural America was like at the turn-of-century.
♥ Pittsburg Chamber of Commerce: 903.856.3442

Wildflower Trails

~ Pittsburg and Jefferson are great starting points to experience the thousands of varieties of blooming wildflowers that paint the countryside with brilliant colours in late April. If you follow the circle created by highways; 49, 11, 125 and 248 you can turn this into an unforgettable drive by packing a picnic basket and stopping at a roadside park to enjoy the view. On the last weekend of April, the towns of Avinger, Hughes Springs and Linden celebrate Wildflower Days and have an assortment of events that include treasure hunts, parades and a great Picnic in the Park in Avinger. Call 903.6397519 for more information.

♥ About one mile North of Linden on Highway 59, there is a sweet little gift shop that is a must. Sweetwater Junction ~ 903.756.5892! Great prices and an amazing selection of "Romantic Gifts" make this a perfect destination spot (Tell 'em Ken sent you!).

The Carson House Inn & Grill

A pleasant surprise in the heart of Pittsburg, this intimate Bed & Breakfast has a charming restaurant that inspires a Romantic Rendezvous. A true sense of history is part of this home that was built in 1878. There were four owners in the course of the first eleven years until it was purchased by William Henry Carson when he moved in with his entire family in 1888.

Mr. Carson was in the lumber mill business and had access to many unique woods. In 1898 he remodeled the house and added Curly Pine base boards, fine carvings, trim and wainscoting to all of the rooms. An intricate scrollwork is over the bay window. This beautiful wood, originally from Louisiana, is now extinct. The Carson House is one of the few places it is known to exist.

Six guestrooms are beautifully appointed in turn-of-the-century antiques and they include the Blue Room, the Oak and White Room and a large two room suite with a private entrance, a king size bed and two twin beds. All rooms have a private bath. In the back of the property is a Railroad car that has been converted into a guestroom. This one-of-a-kind room has a deck around it, a window that overlooks the garden, and a Jacuzzi.

The parlor has a beautiful fireplace and is the ideal excuse to spend a romantic evening at the cozy table in the bay window. Outside, adjacent to the Railroad Car, is a Jacuzzi which allows you the opportunity to enjoy a starlit night or a casual afternoon.

The restaurant has a comfy indoor dining area, and an outdoor patio, nestled in the garden area, is truly magical on a warm night. Begin your meal with Artichoke Dip, Baked Brie, or scrumptious Escargot. A house Raspberry Vinaigrette salad dressing is to live for and entrees include a delicious Pork Tenderloin with a Dijon Demi Glace' sauce, the Sante Fe Chicken is very tasty and has a very colourful presentation and a special version of Chicken Fried Steak incorporates a better cut of beef and a lighter batter. The New York and Filet Mignon steaks are center cut and extremely popular. Lunch is also served, the Sunday Lunch menu includes a generous buffet for only $6.95.

THE CARSON HOUSE INN & GRILL

Guestroom rates: $45.00 ~ $85.00 Fri. – Sat., $35.00 ~ $75.00 Sun. – Thurs.
Discounts available for lengthy stays. Major credit cards accepted.
Average price per person: Lunch: $6.00 ~ Dinner: $4.50 ~ $17.50
302 Mt. Pleasant Street • Pittsburg, Texas 75686
903.856.2468 ~ Fax: 903.856.0709

Jefferson

Situated on Big Cypress Bayou river, Jefferson was once known as "The Riverport To The Southwest" in the mid 1800s. Elegant stern-wheelers cruised down the river from the Ohio, Tennessee and the Mississippi Rivers before and after the Civil War.

Numerous hotels and B&Bs dot the community and a multitude of gift and antique stores are located downtown. Horse drawn carriages, and the Cypress Bayou Train ride are fun excursions. A historical walking tour of the town includes just about every house in the area. Stop at the Excelsior Hotel and the Historical Society and Museum and then visit The House of the Seasons where daily tours allow you to experience the rich and somewhat ostentatious life-styles of past owners. A tour of the 1844 Freeman Plantation is a fun journey and the Floral Gallery across the street, sells beautiful dried floral arrangements, potpourri, wreaths and specially preserved flowers that look fresh cut. The Stillwater Inn, is a very romantic restaurant for those with an unlimited budget.

In December, the Christmas Candlelight Tour takes you into historic homes that are illuminated with hundreds of candles and adorned with 19th century Christmas decorations. The Chamber of Commerce has an expansive info kit which can be had by calling 903.665.2672

♥ Recommended B&B's in town include Captains Castle, once known as the town's most elaborate bawdy house during the river boat heyday ~ 800.650.2330, Twin Oaks Country Inn on the outskirts of town is a picturesque Southern Plantation on beautifully manicured grounds (a country road adjacent to this property is a great excuse for a romantic stroll into undisturbed, and beautiful country) ~ 903.665.3535 Maison Bayou BB is located on the riverbed of the Big Cypress and is nestled in a 55 acre forest. Cute cabins on the river and three room bunkhouses with kitchenettes are available. Enjoy a horse-back ride for an adventure into Bayou country. ~ 903.665.7600

At night, Jefferson is truly a magical world. The streets are empty of people and the lights of the individual homes add a charming touch to the neighborhood. With a full moon high in the sky, you are sure to have "Romance" beckon tonight.

The Charles House

This lovely place is located just a short walk from downtown Jefferson. A two story, turn of the century Dutch Colonial Revival, this house was one of the few of its kind built by the main developers of this area. Comfortably situated in a quiet and peaceful neighborhood, a wraparound porch looks out onto an expansive front yard with towering Pecan trees.

Owner Page Sugg and her official greeter, Jack, the Golden Retriever, encourage you to make yourself at home and enjoy the comforts of this beautiful property. (Jacks' motto is "The world is a pair of hands!" If you watch closely, you will see he has mastered the art of the "Sympathy Limp").

Three guestrooms portray the comfortable side of the Victorian era. All are decorated with antiques and have a private bath, ceiling fans and cable TV. Room #1 is a cozy setting and has a Queen size brass bed, there is a clawfoot tub at the foot of the bed with a heart shaped Venetian mirror above it – an unforgettable romantic encounter! Room #2 has a King size bed and is decorated with Victorian blue colours. Room #3 is a large suite and is painted in soft Lavender colours. A beautiful tapestry sofa and plush down comforters on two queen size beds contribute to the cozy ambiance of this room. The angles of the ceiling allow for an unusual visual experience and a clawfoot tub is a true inspiration to romance.

On a lazy day, doing nothing is time well spent at this B&B. Cozy up on the sofa in the sunny living room and read a good book or, sneak back to your room and enjoy a bubblebath and afternoon nap. In the evening, settle in the rocking chairs on the porch and take pleasure in a Texas evening. Pets and kids are welcome here and smokers can take advantage of the scenic views from the porch.

THE CHARLES HOUSE
Guestroom rates: $85.00 ~ $100.00
209 E. Clarkville Street • Jefferson, Texas 75657 • 903.665.1773

Baker Street Inn

A warm and charming property that stands out from other Jefferson B&B's, as you approach this quaint home, you will see a John Wayne Flag, and American Flag, on the porch, gently waving in the breeze.

Three generations of family have lived in this home built in 1856, and it is currently occupied by Ms. Beth Meyer. With a setting reminiscent of "Grandma's House", this is a great opportunity to "wind down" after your busy day in town. In the morning, Beth serves a full Southern style breakfast on elegant China accompanied by beautiful silverware and crystal.

Two intimate rooms include; *Grandpa's Room* which has original 1800 furniture and a crystal chandelier, and *Myrnie's Room*, with a Mahogany dressing table, gold leaf mirror, and beautiful mahogany window cornices with intricate inlays. Each room has a television and private bath.

Furnished in unique antiques, an afternoon can be spent discovering an assortment of one-of-a-kind collectibles. Start in the parlor which has a hand carved mahogany table and an Imperial Game Table from the 1700's, then step into the John Wayne room, complete with a billiards table. Here you can delight in a variety of memorabilia that pays tribute to this famous actor. Afterwards, relax in the parlor and watch a classic movie on video.

Whatever you chose to do while in Jefferson, the friendly, down-home hospitality of this B&B ensures that your stay is a memorable one. Enjoy!

BAKER STREET INN
Guestroom rates: $85.00 • Monday ~ Thursday: $70.00
409 East Jefferson • Jefferson, Texas 75657 • 903.665.3662

Lake O' the Pines ~ This is a fun late afternoon driving excursion though rolling hills of pine trees and picturesque fields. There are a couple of parks that offer great sunset views on the water and if you keep a keen eye out for the Tejas Village signs, you will discover a once popular resort nestled in the forest that overlooks the lake ~ very romantic around sunset! From Jefferson, take Hwys. 49 to 729 and turn left on 726.

Hale House Bed & Breakfast

Enjoy old-world charm at this beautifully restored Greek Revival B&B originally built between 1868 and 1872 by the parents of May Belle Hale. In 1930 the Hale's expanded the house to accommodate travelling men and women looking for riches in newly discovered oil in east Texas.

The six distinctive guest rooms are decorated with period antiques, ceiling fans, handmade quilts, bathrobes and have private bathrooms with claw foot tubs and showers. For that little extra touch, bath salts, oils, fragrances and blow dryers are provided.

Room 1 has a queen size, wrought iron French Canopy bed draped in French lace and overflowing with pillows, *Room 2* is cozy with a day/trundle bed and bathroom incorporated in the room. *Room 3* boasts style and fashion of the 1800s with period clothing and accessory pieces accenting the six foot carved headboard of this American oak queen bed. *Room 4* is bright, vivid and lovey with an antique white four poster Shaker bed and feather pillows, *Room 5* whispers romance with a fireplace at the foot of the antique queen bed and *Room 6* is warm and spacious with a queen rice bed and comfortable chaise. Perfect for those literary evenings.

Guests are invited to enjoy the parlor, library or the sun porch with wicker furniture, big screen TV and lush greenery. While relaxing on the side porches or gazebo, you will notice that the shape of the bell tower on the Episcopal church opposite the adjacent park is incorporated into the archway of the fence.

Just a few minutes from the historic Austin Street district, Hale House is an ideal setting for small intimate weddings, receptions and gatherings. The relaxed quiet atmosphere is just right for meetings and seminars.

Whether it is business or pleasure, you can expect the special attention you deserve when you visit Hale House Bed and Breakfast.

Guestroom rates: $75.00 ~ $90.00
702 South Line Street • Jefferson, Texas 75657
903.665.8877 ~ Fax: 903.665.2419

Jefferson Best Western Hotel

This is a great place to stay in order to become familiar with Jefferson. Because of the large number of B&Bs in town to choose from, at times it is more convenient to pick one at a leisurely pace. Staying here allows you that opportunity! 65 newly redecorated suites and rooms have TV, telephone and private bath. Jacuzzis are featured in select rooms and an outdoor pool is a nice break on warm day. The Plantation Restaurant has an affordable family style menu and a salad bar, and is decorated in antique furnishings and tables. This hotel overlooks a beautiful grove of trees and a rural "Local" road that takes you into Jefferson, only four blocks away.

A high standard of excellence, friendly staff and comfortable and clean accommodations put to shame the alternative budget lodging in town. If you are on a tight budget, rest assured, you are in good hands!

Guestroom rates: $50. – $96.00 ~ Corporate rates available.
400 South Walcott • Jefferson, Texas 75657 • 903.665.3983

Here is another Great driving excursion: Take 134 South to 20 East into Louisiana and explore the American Rose Center 318.938.5402. You will find thousands of varieties of roses and beautiful garden displays throughout. Head back to 134 North and stop at T.C. Lindsey & Co. in Jonesville. This General Store has been in operation since 1847 and you will find antique collections and hard-to-get items in an old-fashioned setting. Purchase some cheese and Sarsaparilla and then drive east on road 1998 and visit the beautiful cemetery in Scottsville.

This serene setting has many headstones dating from the 1800s and weatherworn by time. A life size marble angel weeps over a young mans grave who died in Mexico in the early 1900s. It reflects the sorrow his parents must have felt at his passing and the ending of the family name. In the wooded area across from the cemetery, pathways and a small pond entice you to enjoy these peaceful surroundings.

Now comes the adventure... Head into Marshall and have a pleasant lunch in the country setting of Stephanie's Restaurant at 500 E. Houston Street ~ 903.927.2544. Ask anyone in town for directions to Stage Coach Rd. This hard-packed red dirt road cuts through a forest and is truly a marvelous drive. If you have ever wondered what it would be like to cross the country in a stage coach, this is you chance to gain a newer appreciation. What a trip! After this journey, take 134 to...

Caddo Lake in Uncertain, Texas

Another area that is easy to get to from Jefferson, a visit to Caddo Lake should be on your "Must Do" list! This ancient lake has thick forests of bald cypress trees growing on small islands or, jutting from the middle of the lake. Many of these trees are 250 to 400 years old and are characterized by a flat top and gnarled appearance.

A tangle of aquatic plants and lush vegetation turn this lake into a maze of sloughs, bayous and ponds. The beauty of this body of water has been ensured by environmentalists world-wide and include singer Don Henly of The Eagles. The Caddo Lake State Park has camp sites and cabins with indoor showers. You can picnic, canoe, fish, hike or launch your boat from this area. 903.679.3351

The roads in and around Caddo Lake inspire an afternoon excursion. If you run across Lighthouse Grocery Store, stop in and have a beer on the picnic tables and tell owners Cecil and Ruth that Ken said Hey! If you are searching for a unique leather wallet or belt, you will find some handsome handcrafted pieces here for which this author now places special orders.

Caddo Lake Steamboat Co. ~ If you have ever been on the riverboat at Disneyland, or wondered what it would be like to ride on an authentic paddleboat, here is your chance to take a step into the past. Relax on the bow of the paddlewheel steamboat; The Graceful Ghost, as owner Lexi Palimore, gives you a narrated tour while expertly guiding you through the scenic and mysterious waters of Caddo Lake. ♥ 903.789.3978

Mystique Tours ~ Should you desire a tour unlike any other you have taken, David Applebaum, a Caddo Lake native, shares his extensive knowledge of these waters as you tool around in his powerboat. Discover the unspoiled beauty of Big Cypress Bayou, the Big Lake area, and the swamps, you just may see one or two gators'. This is a great gift for those who enjoy photography, birdwatching and fishing. If you have romance in your hearts, night tours are available. Ooooohh! ~ 903.679.3690

Looking for a place to eat while in the area?

Big Pines Lodge ~ 903.679.3466 and Bayou Landing ~ 903.789.3394, serve filling portions of steaks and Catfish.

Breakfast at Crips Camp ~ 903.789.3233, is a great way to begin your day.

Waterfront Restaurant ~ 903.679.3957, serves sandwiches, salads and seafood for lunch.

Whispering Pines Lodge

"Another Day in Paradise" is the only way to describe the beauty of this "Old Southern" style brick house located on the shores of Caddo Lake. Built by Victor and Cindy Williams, (the perfect hosts) they have created a soothing environment that sets your mind at ease with each passing day. Suddenly, you don't want to leave!

Three rooms are located in the house; one has a fireplace and all have ceiling fans, TV and an individual bath. The private guest cottage has a ceiling fan, a really neat brick shower, sitting area and TV. A comfy sofa and a king size bed overlook the fireplace – a true inspiration on a cold winters' night. A full Country Breakfast is served in the dining room, adjacent to a large common area with a picturesque view of the lake.

If their schedule allows, Victor or Cindy will be happy to give you a tour of the lake in their powerboat. This unique perspective of magical Caddo Lake shouldn't be missed!

As your day progresses, relax with a good book on the back patio, or on the pier, and take in the scenic views of the lake and the bald cypress trees as a paddleboat gently chugs by in the calm waters. Adjacent to the pier is a cozy brick house that has large screens instead of windows and a double bed which may inspire an afternoon or evening nap. Watch an early morning sunrise or a full moon rise over the lake from this vantage point for a perfect Romantic Rendezvous.

A truly unforgettable place, a day spent under the clear blue skies of Whispering Pines Lodge becomes, "Just Another Day In Paradise!" Enjoy!

WHISPERING PINES LODGE
Guestroom rates: $95.00
Route 2, Box 51, Karnack, TX 75661 • 903.789.3919

North Central Texas

How do I love thee?
Let me count the ways.
I love thee to the depth
And breadth and height
My soul can reach...

~ Elizabeth Barrett Browning

Texas Sunsets

As the sun sets over Texas, prepare to witness some of the most stunning displays of artwork nature has to offer. At dusk, it's hard to fathom how the sky can hold all those brilliant colours on one canvas. Mandarin orange, violet, cobalt blue, yellow, and fuchsia pink melt together, completely taking over the western skyline. As the sun sinks completely from view, the colours intensify. Any clouds on the horizon become backlit by sparkling tones of molten silver and gold. There's never a bad seat in the house to watch this kaleidoscopic phenomenon take place.

Waxahachi
(pronounced: Wok-saw-hat-chy)

A marvelous escape from the city is only 35 minutes from Dallas/Fort Worth, this vibrant community has beautifully restored Victorian home and a charming downtown with a unique building; The Ellis County Courthouse. Built in 1894, this grandiose brick and granite structure shows off an assortment of intricate carvings incorporated into its facade. Upon closer examination, you will find assorted animals and face carvings of young women, (one is of a local love interest of artisan/sculptor Harry Herley and young men (one resembles ol' Beelzebub).

The roots of this town began in 1846, later when the cotton business was booming, farms spread across the county and streets were paved where the buffalo and the longhorns used to roam. Many movies have been filmed here, including Bonnie and Clyde, Tender Mercies, and Places in the Heart. Today the town is a "sidewalk museum" with one of the largest concentrations of Gingerbread Victorian and Period architecture in the state.

A tremendous wealth of architectural treasures is yours to enjoy as you explore the area. For an unforgettable adventure, bicycle the back streets in the Spring or Fall. Watch a stage production at the restored Chautauqua Auditorium located in Getzendaner Park (many notables took the stage here including Will Rogers and William Jennings Bryan). The Ellis County Museum showcases hundreds of antiques and historical artifacts.

Notable annual event include: The Gingerbread Trail which offers guided tours through mansions and manors built by cotton barons, Scarbourough Faire is a Renaissance Festival that takes place in the Spring, A Faire on the Square each Thanksgiving weekend, is a Victorian Christmas celebration held in the downtown square that includes horse and buggy rides as well as guided tours of the Ellis County Courthouse. The Waxahachie Triathlon is recognized as one of the best three Triathlons in Texas. Chamber of Commerce: 971.937.2390

The Dove's Nest Restaurant ~ is adjacent to a spacious antiques shop which you can explore before or after lunch. Four star delights are served (at reasonable rates) and include The Chicken Apricot Salad, Spinach Salad, and the Veggie Classic Sandwich. The Orange Spice Iced Tea is quite delicious. This setting is truly romantic at night. Average price per person: Lunch: $5.00 –$7.00 ~ Dinner: $13.00 – $25.00
♥ 105 Jefferson Street ~ 972.938.3683 (DOVE) ♥

Catfish Plantation Restaurant ~ A cozy Victorian structure whose claim to fame is not just an excellent menu, but its three resident ghosts. Don't be afraid, these are friendly ghosts who oversee the preparation of some of the best Cajun food this side of the Louisiana border. For starters, try the Sweet Potato

Patty and the Fried Dill Pickles; sliced pickles lightly battered and friend and served with a buttermilk dip. Yummy! Of course, Catfish is the specialty here and it is served blackened, baked or fried. The Catfish New Orleans is a Creole lovers delight. Fried Quail, Frog Legs, Stuffed Crab and assorted chicken dishes and low-fat dinners are sure to tempt the taste buds. For dessert, try the Blackberry Cobbler. Double Yummy! Average price per person: $9.00 – $!2.00
♥ 814 Water Street ~ 214.937.9468 ♥

Mother Nature's Recipes for Romance

RAINY DAYS AND SUNDAYS

The versatile weather of Texas allows many opportunities to enjoy a Romantic Rendezvous. Search for cozy restaurants with fireplaces and windows that overlook a park or scenic countryside. Keep that info stored in the back of your mind so that when the day comes, you can enjoy a romantic moment over a bottle of wine.

Enjoy an afternoon drive on country roads and find a lake with a nice spot to pull-over and a view of the water. Play a favourite romantic tape, cuddle under a blanket, watch the submarine races and then steam up the windows. An occasional sweep of your windshield wipers will allow for breathtaking views of cloud formations and stunning countryside.

Or just stay at home, bring out your old record collection, or CDs, then make your own personal, romantic tape. Always have on hand a relatively simple puzzle, buy a bottle of champagne and assorted cheeses and sit in front of the fireplace for timeless memories.

And lest we forget... There's a lot to be said for an intimate champagne bubblebath and then snuggling up in front of the fireplace in your "jammies" afterwards. If you're lucky enough to have a big ol' thunderstorm going on in the background with heavy winds and rain, consider yourself fortunate that you have nothing to do but enjoy the company of your sweetheart.

Chaska House

𝓐 delightful surprise just minutes from the town square in historic Waxahachie, the gentle ambiance of The Chaska House is a true inspiration to those in search of romance. Listed in the National Register of Historic Places, this home was built in 1900 by a prominent merchant, Edward Chaska and his wife Marie.

The Chaska House is a beautiful colonnaded structure with a wrap-around veranda, and large rooms with high ceilings, the architectural style reflects the joyous "Revival" attitude that flourished at the turn-of-the-century. An extensive collection of American, English and French antiques inspire detailed exploration.

Guests are encouraged to be at home in the elegantly furnished Grand Hall, Library, Dining Room, and country-sized kitchen. On a lazy afternoon snack on refreshments in the comfort of the beautiful garden or shaded veranda. A casual day can be spent relaxing in the library browsing through a large collection of books and memorabilia. Comfortable chairs may even inspire a nap.

Two guest suites are appointed with special touches guaranteed to win your heart. *The Plantation Room* is a bright corner room with a comfortable sitting area and a tall, queen-sized canopy bed from an antebellum Alabama plantation. To complete a romantic evening, the spacious private bath with a large soaking tub, provides the perfect setting for a candlelight encounter.

The French Room is a warm and cozy side room with an ornate Louis XIV double bed, matching dresser and a French armoire. A private side entrance to the secluded East veranda may inspire a Romantic Rendezvous on a moon lit night.

Contrasting the Victorian charm of Chaska House is *Hemingway's Retreat*, a guest house just a few steps away. This romantic cottage is decorated to capture the simple declarative flavour of Ernest Hemingway's Key West and Cuban homes.

Created for an extended stay (two days or longer) it is arranged as a one and two bedroom duplex, each with its own living area, kitchen and private bath. Both overlook the peaceful pecan-shaded courtyard garden filled with blooming shrubbery, flowers and comfortable chairs. The Caribbean ambiance is an inspiration to those seeking solitude and "island" romance in the heart of Texas.

Guests are invited for a full southern breakfast elegantly served in the formal dining room of the Chaska House, A delicious "Texas Chic" breakfast may include Stuffed French Toast Strata, Feta Fritatta, Romeo & Juliet, Eggs a la Canoe and more.

A casual stroll to the town square provides a fine adventure to enjoy a museum, antique shopping and good restaurants. A true inspiration to the "Art of Romance", The Chaska House is favourite place to visit anytime of the year.

CHASKA HOUSE
Guestroom rates: $90.00 ~ $125.00
716 West Main Street • Waxahachie, Texas 75165
972.937.3390 ~ 800.931.3390

Love Note...

Downtown Waxahachie is a wonderful excursion once the streets roll up around 5:00pm. The majestic courthouse seems to stand guard over the quiet streets and you may find yourselves talking in whispers as you window shop and admie the old buildings. Let you imagination go and reflect on what it was like when this town was booming in the late 1800s.

Romantic Texas · 33

The Harrison Bed & Breakfast

Another beautiful Bed and Breakfast in historic Waxahachie, as you step onto the veranda and enter the Grand Entry Hall you will feel as if you have traveled to England where this stately mission bungalow architectural style became popular.

Built by James Wright Harrison for his bride in 1915, Mr. Harrison was an incredible man with an obsession for precision and symmetry. He weighed each and every brick before it was laid, knowing that over the years, if you put a heavier brick on top of a weaker one, it would crack. Needless to say, there are no cracks in the home or foundation.

The home is noted as being one of the finest turn-of-the-century homes built in all of north Texas. In the 1900s when basements were set away from the house, Mr. Harrison built not just a basement under the house, but a civil defense shelter, in anticipation of an occasional tornado. Truly a man ahead of his time!

Owners Mark and Sandee Larkin take great pleasure in inviting you into their home and have taken great care in decorating three well appointed rooms that display exquisite European antiques, family heirlooms and "Harrison history".

The spacious Harrison Suite is connected with the study and is draped and canopied in garnet toile fabric. Blended with turn of the century walnut antiques, this king-size bed boudoir is a true delight. A private full bath, private entrance from the veranda and a fireplace make this a very special room on a cold Texas night. The Manchester has the grandeur of an English summer home and displays an elegantly canopied four poster queen-size bed that is surrounded by English and French antiques. A private bath has a large sit down shower. The appealing and intimate Rendezvous is a short stroll from the main house and has an antique English queen bed. A clawfoot soaking tub just may inspire your own Romantic Rendezvous!

A gorgeous veranda is an invitation to guests searching for relaxing moments during their stay. Here you can easily spend hours in pleasant conversation with your sweetheart, reading a good book or just watching the world drift by. In the evening, you may see a couple of "Lovebirds" cozying up in the Victorian rockers and then walking hand in hand to the courthouse and town square.

Start your mornings with a gourmet breakfast and think about how you would like to spend your day. Afterwards, settle into a cozy chair in the study, the living room, the sunroom or veranda and savour Sandee's Coffee Chaser Cookies and a cup of gourmet coffee or specialty tea. A hot tub under the rose arbor is an inspiration for romance any time of the day.

Always a pleasure to visit, if you appreciate the relaxing qualities of English country elegance, The Harrison Bed & breakfast is sure to bring a smile to your face.

THE HARRISON BED & BREAKFAST
Guestroom rates: $95.00 ~ $130.00
717 West Main Street • Waxahachie, Texas 75165
• 972.938.1922 ~ E-Mail: Harrison@CyberHighway.net

Fort Worth

A great "little/big" town, Fort Worth has many different areas that are fun to explore. The beauty of The Courthouse is very apparent at night when lit by floodlights, and the Water Gardens near the Convention Center are a nice destination point in the afternoon

Experience the old West at the Stockyards Historical District, a great excursion any time of day. A fair percentage of those who frequent this area take the Old West concept very serious. Don't be surprised to see many of them dressed in period clothing and/or complete cowboy and western gear. Explore the Livestock Exchange and Cowtown Coliseum and the exciting nightclubs that include Billy Bob's Texas and the White Elephant Saloon. Riscky's Sirloin & Saddle Inn (there is more than one Riscky's in the area, this is the most intimate) has the best steaks in Texas and a bar area with cozy booths. Be sure to try the Pecan Pie! 120 Exchange Street. After dinner, take a romantic stroll behind Riscky's in Saunders Park along Marine Creek. If you are shopping for Western Wear, stop at Circle R Ranch Wear at Stockyard Station where you will find some of the best clothes in Texas. (Tell "Sugar", Ken said Hey!) 140 E. Exchange • 817.626.9966. Don't forget to take a ride on the Tarantula Railroad steam train excursion. Miss Molly's B&B is here to tour or to stay (see upcoming review).

Forest Park is a great area to explore in your car or on a bike. You will see many exquisite homes and beautifully manicured lots (Oddly enough, just about all of these homes are built of brick). The City Park Cafe, a San Francisco bistro, is quite popular with the locals and has a relaxing atmosphere that is perfect for a first date. A great Saturday Brunch is a wonderful way to begin your weekend. The food is very good and reasonably priced, the Escargot sauce is great for bread dipping – the Chicken Delights are tasty, too! Forest Park at Park Hill • 817.921.4567. Stop at the Coffee & Tea House, and discover the unique blends of coffee and tea, as well as chocolate goodies and neat gifts. 2970 Park Hill Drive • 817.927.7744

The Cultural District includes the Will Rogers Memorial Center, which features many equestrian contests, musicals and year-round events, the Fort Worth Museum of Science and History, Amon Carter Museum, the Modern Art Museum and the Kimbell Art Museum named "America's best small museum", features works by Rembrandt, Cézanne, Picasso and other notable artists. 3333 Camp Bowie Blvd. • 817.332.8457.

Another noteworthy museum in downtown Fort Worth is the Sid Richardson Collection of Western Art

The Fort Worth Zoo is a fun excursion 817.871.7950. The Botanic Garden, the oldest in Texas, contains more than 2,500 native and exotic species of plants in 110 acres of garden and natural settings. Highlights of this park include the Rose Gardens, Exhibition Greenhouse and Conservatory. The Japanese Gardens are quite beautiful, one of the nicest this author has ever seen. Be sure to bring a camera, along with that special someone.

Sundance Square is a night time hot spot where you will find a great mix of restaurants, coffee houses, bars and nightclubs. The western cowboy theme is less apparent here, and it appeals more so to the casual business person and/or Generation X'rs (for lack of a better word). If you want to be in the heart of the scene, consider lodging at ...

The Worthington Hotel

An expansive property that has recently undergone a multi-million dollar renovation, this hotel is a real showplace and a stimulating atmosphere for the weary business person. Oversized guest rooms are designed with quality and taste in mind and built with angled walls. The large picture windows frame stunning views, especially at night. Custom fabrics, rich woods and warm colours combined, portray a distinct ambiance. The Athletic Club features a complete fitness center, indoor swimming pool, hydrotherapy pool and two rooftop tennis courts. A variety of restaurants are available for the discriminating guest, including Reflections and the Star of Texas Grill; a great Sunday Brunch is served on the bridge of the Marketplace. The second floor Lobby Bar seems to float in the air as live piano music warms the spacious interior of the hotel.

• Request a room with an Easterly view during the full moon phase, and take pleasure in a lunar sensation as it rises above the city skyline. This is a very romantic way to begin a night-on-the-town as you sip wine or champagne with your significant other.

Guestroom rates: $160.00 – $190.00
200 Main Street • Fort Worth, Texas 76102
• 817.870.1000 ~ Fax : 817.338.9176

Miss Molly's B&B

Historic Accommodations of Texas

As you open the etched glass door and ascend the stairs to the second floor, its like walking into the Old West. You arrive at Miss Molly's in the middle of a turn-of-the-century parlor illuminated by a central stained glass skylight. Built in 1910 and operated originally as a prim and proper rooming house, this historic second floor became a popular "Bawdy House" in the 1940s named the Gayette Hotel.

Operating in the true Bed & Breakfast tradition, the hotel offers eight rooms furnished in Old West antiques – typically a double-sized iron bedstead and an oak wash stand with ceramic bowl and pitcher, and appointed with lace curtains and handmade quilts. Seven of the rooms share three bathrooms "down the hall", each private with iron tubs, pull chain toilet and pedestal sink. Although this author isn't often responsive to shared baths, its not a concern here. After a nice soak in the bubbles, put on the custom bathrobe graciously supplied for all guests, and just enjoy the pleasing and unique surroundings of your authentic journey to the past.

The rooms include; Cattleman's, with a carved oak double bed situated below the mounted longhorns on the wall (what a headboard!), Rodeo, with pictures, posters and a trunk of rodeo paraphernalia and The Gunslinger, which has photographs of famous and infamous gunslingers who have frequented Fort Worth. Miss Josie's, (named in honor of the former madam of The Gayette Hotel) is the premier room, and is decorated in a Victorian manner with elaborate wall coverings and window dressing. Draped fabric covers the ceiling and hangs above the carved oak furniture. A unique private bath inspires an unforgettable Romantic Rendezvous.

Breakfast is served in the parlor beneath the stained glass skylight where guests can enjoy coffee, tea, juice, fresh fruit and hearty specialty breads while they read the paper or visit with the other guests. This is a very nice way to begin your day as you enjoy your stay in the history of the Fort Worth Stockyards.

Guestroom rates: $95.00 for rooms with shared baths; $170 for Miss Josie's room - Special rates available Sunday ~ Thursday.
109-1/2 West Exchange • Fort Worth, Texas 76106
• 817.6261522 ~ 800.996.6559

Pearl Street Inn

A stately, two story 1912 Prairie style home, the asymmetrical facade of this Bed and Breakfast emphasizes wide eaves, horizontal lines, large square porch supports and a massive wood front entry door.

Four guestrooms have beautiful Victorian touches; The English Garden Suite displays a king-size white iron and brass bed, The Estes Room beckons you with an antique American Victorian bedroom set, The Pink Rose Room includes an 8 ft. tall Belgian Eastlake bed and crystal lamps, and the Pearl Room envelopes you with its subtle tones and has an 1890 Victorian bed with lace valances. Dee Dee's Room is an Art Deco/Art Nouveau design with bold colours and a pink marbleized headboard.

Breakfast includes specialties such as Apricot Spice French Toast, Pearl Pumpkin Pancakes or Baked Green Eggs (and ham?). A comfortable living room has a TV/VCR and stereo system for guests, or you can assemble puzzles and play board games at the spinet desk in the airy den. Relax and reminisce on the front porch or in the screened side porch and then explore historic Granbury only two blocks away — the perfect excuse for a romantic stroll with your sweetheart.

Guestroom rates: $79.00 ~ $ $98.00
319 West Pearl Street • Granbury, Texas 76048
• 817.279.PINK (7465) ~ 888.PEARL ST (732.7578)

Granbury

Step into the past when you visit the historic town square and savour the small town charm of downtown Granbury. Search out over 50 antique galleries and gift shops and then discover the grand old Victorian homes in the area.

The 1886 Opera House presents musicals, plays and original productions while the The Chrysalis Cultural Center, once a small country chapel, showcases musical performances. Lake Granbury offers an array of watersports, where you can ski, fish, swim or sail. A great romantic adventure is yours when you ride the Mississippi River style paddle wheeler. In mid-September, the General Granbury Civil War Reenactment depicts battles and skirmishes that took place during the career of Granbury's namesake. Convention & Visitors Bureau: 800.950.2212.

Glen Rose

A charming little area with plenty of country roads to explore, a Nuclear Power Plant brings a fair amount of government money into Glen Rose and Sommervell County. Consequently, the schools and city buildings are new and very nice. Downtown Glen Rose is fun to explore on a lazy afternoon. The 1893 Sommervell County Courthouse has a large star shaped drinking fountain with mineral waters that are supposed to have healing powers. Many of the native fossilized wood buildings are historical landmarks. Enjoy breakfast, lunch or dinner at ME Corral (great prices!).

Squaw Valley Golf Course is a duplicate of the Wee Saint Andrews golf course in Scotland and it is like being on the famous moors. 800.831.8259. The majestic Texas Amphitheater is a great place to go for quality outdoor concerts,

pageants, musical, plays and July 4th the stars (be sure to bring a picnic to enjoy one of the grassy areas). 800.545.6018 Every Friday and Saturday evening from June through October, "The Promise", a musical drama reflecting the life of Jesus offers inspirational entertainment in a beautiful evening setting. 800.687.2661

A "Must Do" adventure: Drive through Fossil Rim Wildlife Center's Scenic drive that takes you through wooded hills and African-like savannahs. This free-roaming environment give you the chance to see and feed exotic, threatened and endangered animals in expansive pastures. And giraffes will stick their head through your car window in search of goodies! Prices: $.9.95, Children, Adults, $12.95, Seniors $11.95 ~ 817.897.2960

The Art Of Dating

In the beginning of any relationship, many people look for reasons why "it can't work" before they consider why it can. Everybody has commendable qualities and if you spot some on the first or second date, consider yourself fortunate and try to find out more about that person.

A positive outlook is a good sign, looking for the bad is disheartening. Consider a potential relationship with an open mind, look for the best in people with the belief that their lessons in life, right or wrong, have created a sensitive person worth knowing

Lily House

An unexpected pleasure in Glen Rose, this recently restored 1870 Victorian mansion sits elegantly on a hill with panoramic views of the area. Multi-colour trim accents the fine lines of the house, a very visual experience for those who appreciate turn-of-the century architecture.

Upon entering, you will see a beautiful staircase, and upstairs is a well-stocked library with a multitude of books. Upon further inspection, you are sure to appreciate the labor of love that owners Bob and Renita Carpenter have put into this restoration.

Three guest rooms in the main house have private baths, high ceilings with ceiling fans, individual climate control and sitting area. Two rooms have fireplaces and an old fashioned claw foot tub. Antiques are found throughout. The Rose Room displays Waiverly wallpaper and linens, and a Victorian love seat that Bob's grandmother brought across the country in a covered wagon. Mr. Bucks room has a fireplace, Eastlake twin beds with six foot high headboards, matching Murphy bed and a ship's washstand in the bathroom.

The two room Carriage House is both lovely and unique. The Sky Room is on the first floor and has a large cedar post bed and a big native stone shower. The Treetop is a colourful, soothing room on the second floor that looks out on a hackberry tree that is always filled with chirping birds. A whirlpool tub offers a relaxing break from the world.

Breakfast is served family style at a large table that seats twelve. Beautiful leaded glass windows in the kitchen allow the morning sun to brighten up your day. Or, enjoy your meal on the porch with the beautiful views of the terraced hillside. A small glass enclosed back porch with plants is a nice escape any time of the day.

Some Friday nights, a special event takes place here. Bob and Renita are professional storytellers and guests are sure to delight in an unforgettable encounter. Enjoy!

LILY HOUSE
107 Lily Street • Glen Rose, Texas 76043
817.897.9747

Love Note...

After your dishwasher has cleaned the dishes, put a note in one of the glasses that tells your partner you will put the dishes away. This is sure to bring a smile to their face!

Hummingbird Lodge

An enchanting way to enjoy a taste of Texas, a visit to Hummingbird Lodge is an adventure to a peaceful scenic paradise. As you drive down the country road to the lodge, you will pass a forest of towering cedars and oak trees and a pond with geese enjoying a sunny day. Here is a little slice of heaven that is sure to win your heart.

Just around the bend is a two story contemporary lodge designed by architect Richard Fowlkes who resides here with his wife Sherry, a retired schoolteacher. They invite you to enjoy their dream home that is nestled on a hillside, overlooking the expansive 140 acre property

Relaxing moments are in store for you as you walk in the fields, fish in the stocked pond and discover the numerous paths that lead through the forest. Here you will find hand built timber bridges, the clear pools of Waterfall Creek and secluded picnic spots. The wildlife includes deer, turkey, wild birds, scampering squirrels and of course... Hummingbirds. No need to worry about getting lost, hand painted signs point out beautiful sights, and directions to the lodge.

Two guestrooms are in the lodge and another four are in the adjoining building next door. All are comfortably decorated and have private baths. A laundry room is available and a refrigerator is stocked with a an assortment of "Honor" sodas and bottled water. A continental-plus breakfast served in the morning in the large dining room includes fresh coffee, cereals, pastries, fruit and a main dish. Be sure to stop at the store in Glen Rose to pick up fixins' for a picnic or dinner and take advantage of the kitchen facilities or outdoor barbecue. Evenings are the start of something wonderful and can begin on the front patio while watching a beautiful sunset, then, relax in front of the fireplace in the main living room and enjoy this peaceful setting with picture windows, gentle moving ceiling fans, soft lighting and under the beamed cathedral ceiling. A separate game room allows you the opportunity to spend quality moments with your sweetheart.

The true pleasure of visiting Hummingbird Lodge is the outdoor hot tub. To get there, walk down a gravel pathway to the wood deck nestled in a small grove of trees. Relax in bubbling water and take in the picturesque views of the adjacent field and forest. As the full moon rises above the trees, an unforgettable Romantic Rendezvous is in store for you! (When this author visited, an unexpected lunar eclipse was taking place, ooohhh!).

A favourite place to visit any time of the year, the serene peace of Hummingbird Lodge will touch your heart for years to come.

HUMMINGBIRD LODGE
Guestroom rates: $79.00 ~ $115.00
P.O. Box 128 • Glen Rose, Texas 76043
• 817.897.2787 ~ Fax : 817.897.3459

Stephanville

A bustling college town, Stephanville is recognized as "One of the Best 100 Small Towns in America". Beautiful golf courses and many open air country activities include horseback riding, swimming, water skiing and tennis. Visit the old courthouse while in town, as well as the Stephanville Historical Museum which has a two room schoolhouse that was built in the 1890s. There is also an historical Church that is an ideal spot for a wedding. At Christmas, check out "Christmas on the Square and in the Park".

There are many retail and antique stores in town and over 50 restaurants to choose from. Montana's has a reasonably priced menu and excellent food and the Dinner Bell serves steak and seafood in one of the oldest homes in Stephanville (it was built in1857). Springtime brings the Native Heirloom Plant Faire and the Chili cook-off, both in April, and a Bluegrass Festival and Antique extravaganza in May. There is a flea market every second and fourth weekend and entertainment at the local stage theater. Chamber of Commerce: 800.658.6490

More Romantic Drives

- A nice drive East of Stephanville and North of Glen Rose: HWY. 56 or 144 offer a stunning view of Comanche Peak. This scenic mesa was once the North boundary of The Comanche Nation.

- Dinosaur Valley State Park, located on the Paluxy River, and off of FM 205, where you can view tracks of two species of dinosaurs made over 65 million years ago. The park also has camping, hiking and swimming (these tracks have bee widely publicized, nationally).

- A country road known as the county's "Lovers Lane" runs along the Paluxy River. This area is especially nice under a full moon. Take FM 205 North from US 67 to Co. Rd. 1008 during the day in search of beautiful scenery and a Romantic Spot, then bring your sweetie back at night.

- Co. Rd. 1008 continues North to Hwy. 51, turn left about a half mile to thee "Ghost Town" of Paluxy where you will find old abandoned store buildings and a church with an historic arbor where revival meetings are still held. Very serene and peaceful.

Oxford House

A beautiful Victorian B&B, minutes from the historic downtown district of Stephenville and Tarelton State University. The romance of this house began when it was built in 1898 by Judge W.J. Oxford for his first wife. Since 1985, Paula and Bill Oxford have worked hard to restore this B&B to its original splendor.

Like visiting Grandmas House, this quaint home is a true step back in time. An historical newsletter about the home and family serves as an inspiration to search out antiques, memorabilia, and family photographs on a casual afternoon. There is an English garden with a gazebo that is quite beautiful in the spring and fall.

Even though there are only four guest rooms, they each have their individual decor and private baths with large, comfy clawfoot tubs, specialty soaps and bubblebath (complimentary homemade chocolate Truffles are left on your night stand). The Marie Suite overlooks the garden, The Bridal Suite has a stained glass window with a seat and is perfect for honeymooners. This room is named after Aunt Mandy because she is said to have been a real character, expecting to be waited on hand and foot whenever she visited, The Oxford Master Suite is a combination of two Victorian rooms with antique marble-topped dressers and an old-fashioned sleigh bed. The Napoleon Room has a blue/gray decor and is named after the first born son.

Candlelight dinners, by reservation are served for guests in the beautiful dining room. This is the perfect spot for a proposal, honeymoon or romantic dinner. Gourmet selections include Beef Tenderloin with Burgundy Sauce, Oxford Chicken with White Wine Tarragon Sauce, homemade pastas and other creative cuisines.

Breakfast may include; pears baked in wine sauce, country sausage biscuits, various egg dishes, German apple pancakes and German cinnamon rolls and French Toast with peach sauce. All homemade, with a touch of love. In the afternoon, fresh baked cookies or sweet breads are in the parlor for all to enjoy. So relax, gear down and take in the serenity of this Victorian Home. It is an experience you won't forget.

OXFORD HOUSE
Guestroom rates: 65.00 - 85.00 per night
Weekday and business rates available during the week.
563 North Graham • Stephenville, Texas 76401
• 817.965.6885 •

Buying the *Right* Rose for the *Right* Occasion

Roses represent many thoughts and occasions.
Here is a list to ensure a befitting presentation.

♥ RED ROSES ♥
Say "I Love You!" They also stand for respect and courage.

♥ WHITE ROSES ♥
Are given to those you adore.
They convey reverence, humility, innocence and purity.

♥ YELLOW ROSES ♥
Are celebrations of life and reflect joy.
Appropriate for new mothers.

♥ CORAL & ORANGE ROSES ♥
Expresses enthusiasm and desire.

♥ PINK ROSES ♥
Embody grace and gentility.
Use **Medium Pink** to say "You're Lovely"
Deep Pink to say "Thank you"
and **Light Pink** to convey admiration.
All pale colored roses stand for friendship.

♥ RED AND YELLOW ROSES ♥
Together symbolize unity.

♥ YELLOW AND ORANGE ROSES ♥
Mixed, stand for passionate thoughts.

♥ PINK AND WHITE ROSES ♥
Arranged together are a sign of enduring love.

♥ THREE RED ROSES ♥
Say "I Love You".

Austin

Love is patient   Love is kind.
It does not envy   It does not boast,
It is not proud   It is not rude,
It is not self-seeking,
It is not easily angered,
It keeps no record of wrongs.
Love does not delight in evil
But rejoices in the truth.
It always protects   Always trusts
Always hopes   Always perseveres
Love never fails...

~1 Corinthians 13:4-8

Austin

A fun city to explore anytime of day, Austin is known for its music, ecology, high-tech businesses, history and liberal outlook on life. The recently renovated Texas State Capitol is a pleasure to visit in the early evening when the area is devoid of people. This is a great place for a romantic picnic in a picturesque setting.

The freeway system is rather questionable in Austin. Even though there seems to be a lot of freeway improvements in the works, traffic doesn't seem to move as it should. Avoid the rush hours and the traffic might move smoothly. If you have a deadline or dinner reservation across town, add an extra half-an-hour to your drive. Just in case!

There are a number of historic sections to discover, including the Capitol, University, and Barton Springs Touring Areas. The Bremond Block Walking Tour and the Hyde Park National Register District are interesting areas to explore. The Elisabet Ney Museum in Hyde Park is a stunning castle-like structure where you can view many of Ms. Ney's sculptures. The Umlauf Sculpture Garden displays over 130 pieces of art by the late sculptor Charles Umlauf in a museum and garden setting. Visitors Info Center ~ 800.926.2282.

A walk down Sixth Street is a year-round Austin tradition. You will find music, shopping, clubs, and other diversions. Also, there are a number of stage theaters in the city producing quality productions. The XL ent, the weekly entertainment section of the Austin-American Statesmen gives up-to-date local entertainment info every Thursday. The Paramount Theatre shows many old movies and the Summer Film Classic series features all-time Hollywood favourites as they were meant to be seen – on the giant screen of a genuine movie palace. Most films are presented as double features and classic Warner Brothers cartoons are an added attraction. 713 Congress Ave.. ~ 512.472.5411

Iron Works Barbecue is a funky little downtown place (it was once a real iron works) built in 1935 that serves great ribs. On a warm day, sit outside on the patio that overlooks a riverbed and a grove of trees. Be sure to buy some barbecue sauce on your way out.~ 512.478.4855

Fairview Bed and Breakfast

Nestled among huge oak trees on the top of a hill, is a beautiful early 1900s Colonial Revival style house with a grand view of this historic neighborhood. As you walk up the steps, two towering trees on either side of the entranceway seem to stand guard over this majestic property.

Carefully restored to its former grandeur by your hosts, Duke and Nancy Waggoner, this home has received numerous awards for historic preservation. Gardens abound and four spacious guestrooms, each with a private bath, are located on the second floor. Exquisite antique furnishings complement the romantic feeling of each room.

The Ambassadors Room features a screened porch that overlooks the front gardens and a full size Eastlake half-tester bed. The Texas Heritage Room displays a king size bed with an impressive high headboard, Texas style! The Back Room has an iron and brass canopy queen size bed with an assortment of lace and floral patterns. And finally, the king size Victorian Renaissance bed in the Governor's Suite is dwarfed by the size of this room which has a large bathroom with a claw foot tub, a separate dressing/sitting room, and beautiful views of the gardens. A double sofa bed in the huge enclosed sun porch is great for an afternoon nap.

The Carriage House has two private rooms that overlook the garden, each with a dining area and a full kitchen. This property is also available for business meetings. A conference room provides a unique setting for private meetings, intimate weddings, luncheons and other small gatherings. Breakfast is served in the Great Room. Afternoon refreshments are offered in the garden, allowing you time to unwind and plan your evening. Consider a night listening to some of Austin's fabulous music venues or just relax under the stars.

FAIRVIEW BED AND BREAKFAST
Guestroom rates: $89.00 – $139.00
1304 Newning Avenue • Austin, Texas 78704
512.444.4746 ~ 800.310.4746 (Reservations) Fax: 512.444.3494

For a very different adventure, the Hill Country Flyer is a vintage steam train that takes you on a journey through small towns and the tree studded countryside of the scenic South San Gabriel Valley. On Saturdays evenings, enjoy a romantic ramble on the Twilight Flyer. ~ 512.477.6377

Romantic Texas · 49

The Governors' Inn

Relive the colourful history of Texas in this 1897 Neoclassical Victorian mansion that was restored to its former glory in 1993. Owners Ed and Lisa Mugford serve up plenty of comfort and charm at this well-appointed estate, you are sure to enjoy many quiet moments during the course of your stay.

A beautiful archway beckons you through carved wood doors with etched glass window panels. Upon entering, you will delight in intricately carved moldings and corners throughout the house. A beautiful wood staircase has 2" etched glass trim, a very unusual and effective display of craftsmanship.

Ten guestrooms, each with a private bath, are furnished with tasteful antiques and are named after a former Texas Governor. Favourite rooms include the Governor Elisha Pease room which has a private porch with (antique wicker chairs) that looks onto large trees and another historical house. The Ma and Pa Ferguson room comes with an interesting Texas story; Pa was impeached for shady business dealings, then Ma ran for his office...and won! She was the first female governor of Texas. The Governor Connally is by far the most romantic room; it has a giant four-poster canopy bed, extensive molding throughout the room and an antique clawfoot tub that is meant for a soothing soak.

Every morning, a gourmet breakfast is served in the elegant dining room. Afterwards, spend a lazy day on the wraparound porches in comfortable Victorian rockers and swings and then picnic under the huge Magnolia tree in the yard. Or, consider a cozy retreat to the parlor which has a beautiful piano that is frequently played by visiting guests.

Only a few blocks from the University of Texas, the State Capitol grounds, and the ever-popular Sixth Street, this Inn is perfect for business or pleasure. Enjoy at your own pace, as Austin has so much to offer.

The Governors' Inn
Guestroom rates: $59.00 – $109.00
1900 David Street • Austin, Texas 78705
512.479-0638 ~ Fax: 512.476.4769

Carmelo's

If you are searching for a Continental dining experience in a romantic atmosphere, this restaurant is for you. Owner and Master Chef Carmelo Mauro invites you to savour the culinary treasures of Italy, his homeland. With two award winning restaurants in Houston and Austin, Carmelo's is winning the hearts of Texans who enjoy fine Italian dining.

A beautiful outdoor water fountain greats you as you enter this establishment. Service is extremely accommodating here and the restaurant is Texas' answer to an authentic Sicilian kitchen, spiced with Continental chic. The tables have white tablecloths, fine stemware, flatware and candles. All combine to set the mood for romance. It is not surprising that many weddings held in the beautiful Piazza are the end result of a romantic dinner here months before.

A scrumptious selection of Italian classics includes appetizers of Escargot, Smoked Salmon, Carpaccio, a house specialty, Black Mussels and Clams, can be served with Marinara, Fra Diavolo or cream sauce. A large assortment of pasta entrees include Liana; a combination of crabmeat, clams and shrimp and garlic sauce, Ravioli Luisa and Pasta Rustica Hilary. Seafood selections include another favourite, Gamberi Ripieli; grilled shrimp stuffed with crabmeat, wild rice and a red bell pepper sauce. Veal, steak and lamb specialties are also part of the menu.

Carmelo likes to keep on the cutting edge with current Italian cuisine and you will be pleased to know that everything is made from scratch (the homemade Italian Sausage is to live for!). This is the perfect spot for a wedding and reception because these facilities can accommodate 10 to 300 people. All under the glow of candlelight!

CARMELO'S
Average price per person $9.75 – $13.95
Austin: 504 East 5th Street • Austin, Texas, 78701
512.477.7497 ~ Fax: 512.477.1620
Houston: 14795 Memorial Drive • Houston, Texas 77079
713.531.0696 ~ Fax: 512.531.0249

Citiview Bed and Breakfast

For these who appreciate the architectural style and inspiration of Frank Loyd Wright, here is a truly unique B&B experience that is sure to leave you with pleasant memories. Built in 1951 on a two acre hillside, this stunning home is accented with original hard-wood floors, high-beam ceilings and wraparound picture windows that offer panoramic views of Town Lake, the Texas State Capitol Dome, the University of Texas Tower and other Austin landmarks. (Recently named "Best View of the City" by the Austin Chronicle)

Two acres of beautifully landscaped grounds feature an English conservatory, swimming pool, Japanese Zen garden and a forty foot Koi pond with a cascading waterfall that ends in a majestic five foot drop into the pond. Nestled on a hillside, this B&B is conveniently located near the city, yet it is off-the-beaten path. Consequently, your privacy and seclusion is guaranteed as you relax in these unique surroundings. Night time is magic as you lounge around the pool or conservatory on a starry evening and steal a kiss under the floral covered gazebo.

Owner Carol Hayden and her husband Ralph Canada are animal lovers and Ralph currently serves on the Board of Directors of the S.P.C.A. in Dallas. Carol founded the "Fur Ball" which is currently the largest fundraiser for animals in Texas and she now serves on the board for the Austin Humane Society/S.P.C.A.

The assortment of exotic animals on the property include Charlie Girl, a blue gold Macaw who has taught herself to answer the phone "Citiview, may I help you?" Phantom the Llama, Nigerian Dwarf Goats, peacocks, bunny rabbits and ducks. In addition, they have three Great Danes, two cats and over 50 varieties of domesticated pet birds.

The three guestrooms at Citiview are the Walnut, Maple and Mahogany rooms.. Each is timeless in design and decorated with a wonderful collection of European Art Deco furnishings imported from Paris. These modern classics date from the 30s, 40s and 50s and keep alive the timeless elegance of truly beautiful furniture designs. The beds are very comfortable and each room has a private bath, television, private phone line, and stereo. Two of the rooms have French doors that open onto a private patio.

No detail has been overlooked in this house, including the birdhouse in the back yard that is a replica of a Frank Lloyd Wright home. A spacious living room and dining area afford the opportunity to relax in pleasant surroundings. Personal daily spa services include manicures, pedicures and massages, plus health club facilities and personal trainer on staff. In the morning, chef Linda Fox, a former chef at Word of Mouth Catering, prepares a gourmet breakfast with the finest organic produce available, often coming right out of the organic garden.

This is the perfect location for any celebration including corporate functions, Fab fifties theme parties, receptions and of course... Weddings! A favourite Romantic Getaway, Citiview B&B is an adventure to unique surroundings rarely found in today's society. Enjoy!

CITIVIEW BED AND BREAKFAST
Guestroom rates:
$149.00 – $169.00
1405 East Riverside Drive • Austin Texas 78741
512.441.2606 ~ 1.800.BST.VIEW ~ Fax: 512.441.2949
http://www.hyperweb.com/Citiview

FAVOURITE AUSTIN RESTAURANTS
Brio is in a 100 year-old Victorian home offering a combination of European and Asian techniques with a touch of local flavor. $10.00 – $19.00 per person ~ 512.499.0442. Jeffrey's, a comfortable setting in a 1932 storefront serves exquisite regional Southwestern food by candlelight. $14.00 – $26.00 per person ~ 512.477.5584. The Cafe at the Four Seasons is in an elegant European atmosphere and serves fine cuisine that combines flavours of Northern France, Germany and a touch of the Southwest. Floral arrangements, subtle earth tones and candles on the table create an intimate setting. Matre'd Shane Briant is one of the best in the city and goes out of his way to ensure a memorable experience for you. $17.00 – $28.00 per person. ~ 512.478.4500. Coyote Cafe is an inexpensive alternative in a casual setting 512.476.0612.

Austin's Wildflower Inn

Nestled in a quiet residential neighborhood of tree-lined streets and well-kept homes, this quaint 1930s two story house is like taking a trip to Grandmas house. Enter though the white picket fence and then into the spacious front porch. You are now in the comfortable surroundings of Austin's Wildflower Inn, where an atmosphere of warmth and comfort is yours to enjoy.

Beautiful oak hardwood floors, antique furniture in every room, handmade quilts and lace curtains are just some of the focal points you will discover when exploring this house. Owners Kay Jackson is a native Texan and invites you to share her dream of owning a Bed and Breakfast.

Are you in the mood for a quiet and relaxing afternoon? The shaded stone patio under the beautiful Texas Oak tree offers seclusion from the world. The bi-level wood deck in the back garden is the perfect way to start your day while enjoying a special breakfast of homemade breads, coffee, fruit and a Wildflower Specialty.

Two of the four guestrooms have a private bath, they are The Canopy Room which has a New Orleans setting furnished with an antique white iron, half-canopy bed, a wicker desk, antique oak rocker and antique lamps. The Lady Pearls Room emits an aura of country charm and has a stately four post oak bed and meticulously stenciled soft blue walls. An antique oak rocker, dresser, library chair, table and daybed complete the warm and cozy atmosphere in the room.

Consider a romantic stroll in the late afternoon or early evening at The University of Texas or State Capitol Complex, both are just a few blocks away or, search out the picturesque surroundings of Shoal Creek Hike and Bike Trail. Afterwards, relax on the front porch and enjoy pleasant conversations with your significant other into the night.

Guestroom rates: $69.00 shared bath ~ $84.00 – $89.00 private bath.
1200 West 22 1/2 Street • Austin, Texas 78705
512.477.9639 ~ Fax: 512.474.4188

The Yule Fest Tree Lighting ceremony in Ziller Park is a noteworthy adventure and offers a great Kissing Spot under the twinkling lights of the towering tree at Christmas time. The National Wildflower Research Center is a great place to explore radiant gardens, a nature trial and indoor exhibits ~ 512.292.4200

Renaissance Austin Hotel

Located just fifteen minutes from downtown and the State Capitol, the Renaissance Austin Hotel features 478 guest rooms and suites which surround a beautiful nine story atrium. Many of the accommodations offer views of the Texas Hill Country.

Trattoria Grande, the hotel's fine dining room, features Northern Italian cuisines and offers great views and atmosphere. The Garden Cafe serves breakfast and lunch in the midst of atrium surroundings. The lobby lounge features weekend entertainment and Tangerines, a high energy nightclub, is a favourite gathering spot for hotel guests and Austinites. For recreation, the hotel offers two swimming pools, an extensive health club, whirlpool and sauna.

This hotel is the cornerstone of the Arboretum, a 95-acre development that includes shops, boutiques and movie theaters. In the early evening or on a moonlit night, take a stroll along the walking paths that lead through the sleek office towers.

Guestroom rates:
$99.00 – $119.00 weekdays ~ $157.00 – $197.00 weekdays
9721 Arboretum Boulevard • Austin, Texas 78759
512.343.2626 ~ 512.346.7953

☆ Lone Star Rendezvous ✶✶✶
Lake Travis & The Highland Lakes

The Renaissance Austin Hotel allows easy access to five major lakes and can allow for numerous hours spent exploring country roads. Lake Travis is the most convenient from this location. A guide with extensive maps is available at 210.263.3188. If you're feeling adventurous, here are some unforgettable country drives:

Begin on 183 South to 1 South. Exit at W. Anderson Ln./Spicewood Springs Rd. and head east on Spicewood Springs Rd. Drive about ten miles on winding country roads. Keep a sharp eye out for St. Edwards Park. Enter the hiking trail and not far from the small waterfall is a rock crossing. Cross Bull Creek, keep to your right and follow the pathway along the cliffs of the river. You'll delight in the pleasures of this serene area. Approximately 3/4 of a mile on your right you will find a small ledge (this may turn into a waterfall after a big rain) with a fifteen foot drop. a great spot to steal a kiss! Directly across the creek from this ledge is a sand bar accessible from a meandering path on the other side of the creek. A great swimmin' hole!

Continue on Spicewood Springs Road to 360 south. Turn right (Northwest) on 2222 to Lake Travis, and turn left on 620. Just before the bridge by Mansfield Dam, pull over to the right, climb the pathway up the rocks and you will have a picture perfect view from high above rocky cliffs. This is a great place to build a small fire and cuddle under a blanket with your sweetie.

Hudson On The Bend

Another great destination point when exploring Lake Travis, Hudson on the Bend specializes in gourmet preparations of wild game. For those who enjoy a break from the standard Texas cuisine, this dining experience is one of the finest in Austin,

The romantic atmosphere is complemented by colourful and eye-catching paintings in an elegant setting. However, the true magic of this property is the outdoor patio which looks onto a pretty garden area, a quaint smoke house and an herb garden. Tiki lamps and twinkle lights in the trees make this a truly wondrous dining experience at night.

Unique appetizers include Omar's Rattlesnake Cakes, (very tasty!) Water Buffalo Enchiladas with rich game sauce and Moulard Duck and Pheasant Liver Paté. This Paté is served with Plum Pistachio Chutney, Mango Jalepeño Marmalade and/or Mexican Marigold Mustard, all guaranteed to please the palate! The menu changes according to availability and may include Antelope, Venison, Seafood, Kangaroo, Grilled Pheasant and Quail. Delicious salads, steaks and seafood are also available and the Mixed Grill lets you sample a variety of game selections. The Backstrap of Javelina stuffed with roasted pecans, and the Grilled Tenderloin of Ostrich are both memorable selections. Each is complemented with a rich Porcini Mushroom Sauce.

If you want to splurge or try something really different, Hudson's On The Bend should be your first choice.

Average Price per person: $34.00 Excluding liquor, gratuity and tax.
3509 Hwy 620 • Austin, Texas 78734 • 512.266.1369

• The following B&B's are two personal favourites in the Highland Lake area...

Trails End B&B

Do you desire a getaway to the country in order to forget your problems and leave the world behind? Trails End B&B is the ideal escape to peaceful surroundings and it is guaranteed to leave an impression in your heart and soul. Located on the top of a hill that overlooks a sprawling valley and forest, the view from this Trails End is truly inspirational.

Your hosts, Tom and JoAnne Patty give you a special kind of attention and encourage you to savour the pleasures of their "Dream House" in a safe and secure, atmosphere.

This two-story house is situated at the end of a gravel road within a country garden setting. The two bedrooms are comfortable and elegantly decorated and offer spectacular views of the surrounding countryside. At night, watch a movie on TV in the upstairs den, or enjoy a cozy moment in the living room by the fireplace. The Treetops Guest House is accessible by stairs that lead through towering trees and inspire thoughts of The Swiss Family Robinson. As you drift quietly to sleep in the comfort of your room, a restful night of sleep is guaranteed.

There are areas that inspire a day of exploration, or just enjoy the solitude and moments of peace that this environment has to offer. Relax in the gazebo, on the sundeck among the trees, or on the observation deck atop of the house, all are ideal Kissing Spots on a moonlit night. During the day, work on your tan by the swimming pool, play a casual game of catch or volleyball in the yard, or consider a two mile bicycle excursion to Lake Travis.

The setting here is a true inspiration for romance and, if JoAnn's schedule allows, she will be happy to prepare a romantic candle lit dinner by the fireplace. In the morning, enjoy an expansive sit-down breakfast in the dining room.

Perfect for anniversaries, weddings or special occasions, this fine Bed and Breakfast allows you to share the pleasures of life with your sweetheart in an extraordinary country setting.

Guestroom rates: $65.00 ~ $95.00
12223 Trails' End Road #7 • Leander, Texas 78641• 512.267.2901

Casa De Esperanza

*H*ere is an experience that is guaranteed to inspire pleasant memories for years to come! This cabin is situated on a private acerage steps away from Lake Travis and is truly heavenly! Constructed in the 1940s shortly before the formation of Lake Travis by the Mansfield Dam, it is built of Texas Limestone and situated under a majestic canopy of over 50 live Oak trees.

Make arrangements with owner Michael and Gail Atwater by phone, and they will meet you at the property at a specified time and then turn over the keys to you.

The cabin has been completely renovated and features A/C, rustic Texas cedar woodwork throughout, and a cozy bedroom. A living room with comfy sofas, stone fireplace and stereo (be sure to bring your favourite romantic CDs) is a great area to unwind any time of the day. A one-of-a-kind shower is lined in fossils found on the shores of the lake and an additional bedroom is at the front of the cabin and has very pretty views of the lake.

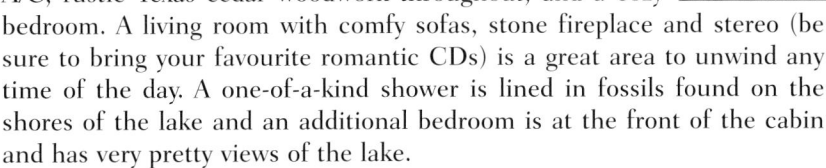

The full kitchen displays many working vintage appliances. A self-serve continental, or a full gourmet breakfast prepared by Gail is yours to enjoy in the dining area which has large picture windows that overlook the lake. Stop at the grocery store before your arrival, and plan a very romantic candlelight dinner in the evening.

The magic of this place is unquestionably its peaceful surroundings. From the front porch, you will see a picture perfect view of a wood fence, a windmill creaking in the steady breeze and gentle waves lapping on the shore. At night, consider a wading in shallow waters or, a moonlight swim. Then, refresh yourself in the private outdoor shower (a true experience at night).

As you have probably guessed, a visit to this cabin can be a true inspiration to the Art of Romance. Located less than an hour from downtown Austin, if you desire an escape to the beautiful Texas country, look no further, you have just found your ticket to paradise.

CASA DE ESPERANZA
21511 Perry Cove • Lago Vista, Texas 78645
512.267.2060 ~ Fax: 512.267.0831

The Texas Hill Country

Love rules the earth,
The grove,
The men below
And saints above

For love is heaven
And heaven love...
~ Sir Walter Scott

Welcome to the Texas Hill Country where open meadows, forested landscapes, sheer cliffs and rolling hills inspire afternoon drives in search of the ultimate picnic spot. A 160 mile radius of exquisite landscapes are resplendent with springs, rivers and lakes, both under and above ground. The Devils Backbone, a four mile stretch of hills that runs between Wimberley and Fischer on Hwy 32, is one of the top 20 scenic routes in Texas

There is a lot of German history in this area, a result of the many immigrants who settled here in the 1800s. Imagine their delight in discovering that even though drastically different from their homeland, Texas had its own natural wonders and unique appeal.

A mix of small towns dot this scenic countryside. All have their own individual character. Lets begin with...

Wimberly

Located on the Blanco River, Wimberley is a quaint country town with two major underground lakes that are said to form a spiritual vortex. Consequently, this area is home to many artists and New-Agers. Throughout the week you will see a variety of people in search of unique art pieces and antiques. Pioneer Town is a reconstructed Old-West town that can be an unusual excursion in the late afternoon or early evening. In the summer, the intimate Opera House has old-fashioned stage productions. On the first Saturday of each month, there is a Market Day. If you go the night before, you may be able to score some good bargains while the vendors are setting up. Grab a couple of beers and have a good time!

☆ Lone Star Rendezvous ✶✶✶

The real beauty of this area lies along the many back roads that take you into unusual parts of the county. Here are a few memorable excursions...

- Take RR12 from the Junction. Head toward town about one mile and on the right is a nice view of the Wimberley Valley. Continue on RR12 to River Road, (with the only street light in town) and take a left on Hilltop Road into Paradise Hills. This is an exclusive neighborhood with homes dotting the hillsides. Park by the intersection of Balance Road and Valley Drive to enjoy panoramic views of the area.

- Follow the river to the low water bridge, take the first left onto Blanco Bend and park in the clearing that has a small covered bridge. Be sure to search out the rock stairs that lead into the woods. This can be an unforgettable Romantic Rendezvous on a spring or summers day; or better yet, at night during a full moon or light rain.

- Enter Woodcreek Resort/Golf Course by the 2325 entrance and take the first right to El Camino Real. The next left is La Forge Trail which brings you to Mt. Baldy. Rock steps inspire a healthy climb to the top of the hill where stunning views are yours to savour. At night, it doesn't get much more romantic than this! These steps were built by the W.P.A. in the 30s and it is said that at one time, there was a jukebox up here. What a trip!

- The outdoor Corral Movie Theater on CR 174 gives you the opportunity to watch movies under the stars in the summer. Bring a lawn chair, blanket and drinks (this is a dry town) and enjoy the pleasure of the Texas night ~ 512.847.2513.

- For an unforgettable expedition, consider a trip to Little Arkansas. A twelve mile drive on semi-paved roads leads you through stunning countryside alongside the Blanco River to a large campgound. Upon your arrival, search out the area by the Goldfish Pond for a contemplative moment in time (this is very pretty in the Spring and Fall). You can spend a day here looking for places to swing and dive into water or, camp out overnight. The campsites are $30.00 per night and all have electricity, picnic tables and access to washers, dryers and showers. Day Pass: $5.00. Directions: 3237 East to Flite Acres, then take 174 across the Blanco River to Camp Howell and follow the "Little Arkansas" markers, (which may be painted on small signs or rock formations).

- The water at Blue Hole on Cypress Creek has a constant temperature of 66 degrees, is crystal clear and comes from 1000 ft. underground. Visit Canyon Lake where the water is so clear you'll see amazing underwater rock formations when snorkeling. You can also rent water skis, windsurfing boards and "Toobs". For more information on the area look for the book Welcome to Wimberley - Now what Do I Do, available at the town bookstore and the visitors center. Visitors Center: 512.847.2201

Love Notes...

Next time you share a bottle of wine or champagne with someone special, sign and date the cork. If you're careful, you might even have room for a little comment about the evening. This makes for a spicy, take-home memento of your time together...and in this case, two bottles are better than one!

Mail a "homemade ♥♥♥♥ Valentine to your sweetheart in AUGUST!! (Or, you can always buy an extra one in February, and save it until you need it).

Blair House Bed and Breakfast

A true Hill Country adventure, this retreat is nestled on 85 acres of beautiful countryside under clear blue skies. As you drive up the tree-lined country road, past the barn, delight in the herd of cattle grazing in the pasture and then the one story ranch house elegantly positioned on the top of a hill.

Upon entering the graciously decorated main inn, you will find a TV room, a spacious living room with a large limestone fireplace and a well stocked library of books, CDs and videos. Choose from seven total guest quarters, all with private baths, some with Jacuzzi tubs.

All rooms have CD players, fresh flowers, chocolates, original art and inspiring views of the Texas Hill Country. The sauna and massage complex is available for all guests to enjoy, professional massage and spa services by licensed therapist can be arranged.

Relax on any number of patios, decks and verandas. Search out deer, red foxes and wild turkeys that come to drink from the pond. Savour a spectacular Texas sunset in the swing or hammock, then sit by the fire outside and gaze at the radiant stars that illuminate the night.

Owner/Chef Jonnie Stansbury takes great pride in preparing multi-course breakfasts featuring fresh organic fruits, produce and homemade cheeses from local farms and dairies. Romantic dinners and picnic baskets are available upon request, and your host will encourage you to search the property for a private picnic rendezvous spot.

An array of desserts served in the evening are guaranteed to delight your palate. The inn offers many special packages including a popular Honeymoon Package that begins with a bottle of iced champagne in your room and... "Breakfast in Bed."

Guestroom rates: $135.00
Route 1 Box 122 • Wimberley, Texas 78676 • 512.847.8828

Southwind B&B

A secluded escape from the demands of civilization, Southwind Bed and Breakfast is nestled in an enchanted world of tree covered hills and picturesque countryside. This quaint, 10 year old, two-story house offers stunning views of a majestic forest and is named for the winds that consistently blow from the south.

Three guestrooms offer undisturbed privacy and include private bathrooms, individual heat/AC units and a private outdoor entrance. A country atmosphere is incorporated into the design of the house which is decorated with antiques and reproduction furnishings. Two rooms have queen beds, one has a king bed and fireplace. In the morning, owner Carrie Watson serves a healthy and natural breakfast.

Two secluded cedar cabins are nestled in the forest. Each have a king bed, a fireplace in the bedroom, whirlpool tub, kitchens, and a swing on the front porch with scenic views of the hills. Bring your favourite foods and take advantage of the cooking facilities in order to prepare a romantic dinner for that special person in your life.

A variety of things to do include hiking, bird and wildlife watching, reading a book in front of the living room fireplace, relax in the quiet seclusion of the front porch, or enjoy the outdoor hot tub that overlooks the valley. At night, the stars are so bright that you just may feel as if you are in the center of the universe. When a full moon shines in the night sky, or if a thunder storm rumbles through the valley and rain falls on the metal roofs, romantic inspirations are guaranteed!

Less than an hour from Austin and a little over an hour from San Antonio and Fredericksburg, Southwind B&B is a safe, relaxing setting without radio or television. Here is the perfect opportunity to savour a peaceful weekend or a restorative night of peace and quiet.

SOUTHWIND B&B
Guestroom rates: $75.00 ~ $90.00
2701 FM 3237 • Wimberley, Texas 78676
512.847.5277 ~ 800.508.5277

Crystal River Inn

The romance of the Hill Country, and the Texas spirit it emanates, are just a part of this two story Victorian house. Built in 1883, it stands out from the neighboring homes. Owners Cathy and Mike Dillon ensure that your stay is an unforgettable one and extend to you a sampling of their down home Southern hospitality.

Sleep until noon and have breakfast in bed, enjoy the rose garden or relax on the veranda in wicker chairs. A courtyard garden area with a fountain becomes more magical at night when the twinkle lights come on. Inside, enjoy the atrium dining room with a piano, wet bar and fireplace, or a comfortable library with overstuffed sofas and chairs. All of these venues can inspire a romantic sojourn any time of day.

Five rooms in the main house have grand designer touches; all are named for famous Texas rivers. Downstairs, the Frio Room and the Pedernales Room have an individualized decor, shared bath and fireplaces, perfect for cool winter nights. Upstairs rooms include: The Medina Room, a honeymoon suite with a majestic four poster bed, charming furnishings and a cozy fireplace; the southwestern themed Colorado Room with Indian rugs, and a canopy bed with a very unusual rope design; and the Blanco Suite featuring a luxurious bedroom that overlooks the veranda, an adjacent room with a double bed, (great for an afternoon nap) and a sitting room with a television.

Two additional Victorian buildings contain suites with other amenities such as telephone, TV, mini kitchens and private entrances. The glamorous San Marcos suite features a king size canopy bed, a fireplace, an extra large marble garden tub, skylight, sitting room and 24-K gold bathroom fixtures.

Celebrate morning in the dining room, or in the garden with a gourmet breakfast. Weekend guests are treated to a memorable brunch with

Bananas Foster Crepes, Eggs Benedict and other excellent specialties. The dining room, fountain courtyard and garden are available for small parties, weddings, private luncheons, dinners and business meetings. Crystal River Inn is famous for its monthly mystery weekends, as well as river trips, romance packages and gourmet cooking lessons.

However you choose to spend your time while visiting Crystal River Inn, rest assured that you will have an unforgettable visit guaranteed to inspire a return in the near future.

CRYSTAL RIVER INN
Guestroom rates: $60.00 ~ $100.00 weekdays
$75.00 ~ $125.00 weekends
326 West Hopkins • San Marcos, Texas 78666
512.396.3739

San Marcos

As you approach the town square of San Marcos, you will see a large courthouse that oversees this quaint Main Street community. Upon further exploration, discover cute shops, antique stores, the enormous San Marcos factory outlet (160 stores) and several brew pubs. A drive, afternoon stroll or evening walk through the back streets of this community can include San Antonio Street, The Courthouse Square and Belvin and Burleson Streets. These National Register historical districts include dozens of beautiful mansions. A historic trolley tour conducted by costumed figures from the city's history takes place on the first Saturday of every month.

Every Thursday in the summer, enjoy Summer in the Park in Veramendi Plaza where you can picnic and listen to music performed in the gazebo. Various musical selections may include classical, jazz, bluegrass, barbershop quartets or symphonic music. Afterwards, take a carriage ride through town and trot the horses through the Beverage Barn for a bottle of champagne.

Check out Mille Seaton's Doll House, a historical mansion whose owners use it exclusively to display a massive collection of dolls, including every Barbie doll ever made (call ahead as hours are irregular) ~ 512.396.1305. The Charles S. Cock House Museum once was residence to former mayors. On Fridays at noon, a San Marcos tradition is to have lunch here, prepared by many locals in costumes.

The San Marcos Riverwalk runs along the San Marcos river and has many great picnic spots, complete with swans floating on the water. During warm weather, inner tubing, canoeing and kayaking are popular activities. Lunch, dinner or Sunday Brunch at Peppers At The Falls offers great vantage points of adventurers "toobing" the Rio Vista Dam. Be sure to search out Children's Park. Although frequented by kids during the day, at night this magnificently lighted playscape draws many over 20 "Kids" who relive their youth while enjoying the slides, swings and the natural river setting.

Wonder World Natural Cave is a great destination point where you can explore prehistoric caves, climb a 110 ft. lookout tower, or enjoy the Petting Zoo, the largest in Texas. Catch a train ride through Mystery Mountain and Crystal Falls – an adventure in itself! ~ 512.392.3760. Aquarena Springs features a small fresh-water lake on a scenic property where you can catch a glimpse of rare aquatic life and scrutinize an underwater archeological site from a Glass Bottom Boat. In the early evening, this is a magical property that has a few choice Kissing Spots. ~ 800.999.9767. The S.W.T.S.U. campus is a nice place to explore at night and a beautiful outdoor ampitheatre, The Glade Theater offers stage productions throughout the year. Visitor Information: ~ 512.396.2495

Devils Backbone Restaurant, located on Hwy 32 has a large fireplace and good food. On Saturdays, you can enjoy live Honky Tonk music. Riley's Tavern has an outdoor patio with great views of the valley and Devil's Backbone. There is a roadside pull off about a mile west that is a great place for a sunset picnic. Other good restaurants include the romantic twinkle-lighted courtyard of Palmer's, and Texas Red's serves huge steaks in a restored cotton gin setting..

Love Notes...

As the sun sets over Texas, early evening puts on an especially romantic sparkle as this town begin to prepare for nightfall. Sunset walks in the parks or quaint old neighborhoods can enhance any special moment in time with your sweetheart.

Write an entry to your "DEAR DIARY" describing a romantic date you fantasize having with him or her. Include every detail and mail it to your sweetie or leave it lying out in a place sure to be discovered.

Gruene

A cute little town with a lot of character, Gruene was founded by German farmers who arrived in Texas in the mid 1840s. Cotton was introduced into the area and by 1870, it was recognized as the number one cash crop. H.D Gruene, (whose home is now a Country Inn in the center of town) had visions of cotton fields spanning the countryside. Unfortunately, because of personal tragedies, the Boll Weevil, and economic disasters in the 20s, this dream never came true. By the early 30s, Gruene was a ghost town.

Life came back to the area in the mid 1970s when new developers realized the value of the existing historic structures. Unique businesses sprang up and now you can browse old fashioned shops, dine at either of four restaurants, and search for antiques in the brick building that was once a mercantile store. Be sure to have your photo taken while wearing authentic Western gear at Smiling Eyes Photo Gallery ~ 629.7474

During the day you can rent an innertube and "toob" the Guadalupe River or, take a whitewater raft, tube or canoe trip with River Outfitters ~ 625.2800 or, Rockin "R" River Rides ~ 629.9999. At night, enjoy dancing at Gruene Hall where you will see many well-known, as well as up-and-coming, stars performing live music. For a unique overnight stay, the Gruene Silo Inn is a one room Bed & Breakfast situated in a medium size silo. This is a very remarkable experience, especially when rain is falling on the tin roof. ~ 210.608.9831

Once the sun sets and the streets are rolled up, a peaceful serenity encompasses the town. Visions of Mayberry enter your mind and a romantic stroll through town is a must! Walk across the bridge, turn left and you will discover an intimate park along the river. With the water tower eloquently lit and a full moon above, this is what The Art of Romance is all about!

Gruene Mansion Inn

A romantic riverside resort, the Gruene Mansion is the crown jewell of the tiny village of Gruene, edged as it is by an elegant white iron fence. This house once belonged to H.D Gruene who founded this town more than 100 years ago. Owners Sharon and Bill McCaskill have gone to great lengths to give their wonderful property a distinctive aura of romance.

25 guest rooms and cottages overlook the Guadalupe River, many are incorporated into restored century-old barns. Spectacular views of the Texas Hill Country from your private deck allows you to savour this magical setting any time of the day. With the river running below and the moon above, it doesn't get much better than this.

These accommodations have been carefully refurbished with a Victorian rustic elegance that is complemented by wrought iron beds with handmade quilts, fine fabrics and wall coverings, antiques, and handmade furniture. Some of the rooms have an upstairs loft accessible by a small staircase. This is a very romantic and inspirational setting. Elegant bathrooms have pedestal sinks, and deep old-fashioned claw foot tubs that fairly whisper "bubblebath".

Although guests don't lodge in the main house, a gourmet breakfast is served in the elegant dining room with fine silverware and flatware. Favourite selections may include Blueberry pancakes or "Eggs A la Gruene Mansion Inn".

This property is another "Lone Star Favourite" and is perfect for honeymoons, anniversaries and romantic getaways. During the week, Gruene is a very quiet area in the evening. You can now enjoy a moonlight stroll in town with that special person in your life.

Guestroom rates: $85.00 – $200.00

Breakfast by
reservation only:
$5.00 per person + tax

1275 Gruene Road New Braunfels,
Texas 78130 210.629.2641
Fax: 210.629.7375

The Restaurant at Gruene Mansion

Nighttime in Gruene should begin with a romantic dinner at this establishment. A large, spacious barn has a rustic setting with wood tables, high beam ceilings and ceiling fans. A stone fireplace and candles on the table set the mood for romance. The waitstaff is very personable and familiar with all dining, and wine selections. Or, you can choose a recommended wine that is listed next to the entrees on the menu.

European Cuisine, combined with Texas favourites, make this an interesting menu with many fun selections. For appetizers, try the Shrimp Royale or the Sauteed Mushrooms that has a great sauce for dipping bread (anything with mushrooms on it is a good choice!). A variety of salads, pasta, seafood, sausage, pork and beef are yours to choose from. The Chicken Poivrade and Chicken Aux Champignons are very tasty, as is the New Braunfels Smoked Sausage and the Jagerschnitzel; traditional German favourites.

Average price per person: $9.95 – $12.95 Excluding liquor, gratuity and tax

1275 Gruene Road • New Braunfels, Texas 78130 • 210.620.0760

New Braunfels

The Official German community of the United States, New Braunfels is situated on the Guadalupe and Comal rivers. A tribute to this German community is the Wurstfest (November 1 - 10) which draws thousands of people in search of authentic German beer and sausages.

The historic downtown area is fun to explore and a variety of excursions can include the Hummel Museum and the downtown antique mall. For a blast into the past, discover the turn-of-the-century Henne's Hardware Store which has an overhead contraption that once transported money from the cashier to the back office.

Rent a paddleboat on the Comal River (the shortest river in the world) and then check out the Arboretum in Landa Park. This park has many hiking trails that lead to out-of-the way picnic spots. The downtown movie theater shows recent releases on two screens and on Fridays and Saturdays, you will see parents dropping off their kids for an afternoon matinee. Watching the kids holding hands and waiting for their parents after the show, is a heartwarming sensation.

Enjoy a cup of Java at The New Braunfels Coffee Shop or, sample fresh baked pastries at Naeglin's Bakery (in operation since 1868). Pat's Place has the best hamburgers in town, Log Haus serves authentic German and Continental cuisine, Keno's Barbecue is a must, and Huisache Grill prepares some of the finest food in town. Chamber of Commerce: 800.572.2626

☆ Lone Star Rendezvous ✦✦✦

Head south on Hueco Springs Rd. and just past the Kuebler–Waldrip House is Whispering Woods Rood, turn right and park at its end. This is a nice moonlight kissing spot or, during the day, explore the woods on your right. Go back to H.S.R. and turn left on River Rd. for a drive through scenic countryside. There are a number of pullover spots here and you can rent rafts or innertubes at Jerry's Rentals or Riverbank Outfitters, or, enjoy a fun drive through the Natural Bridge Wildlife Ranch next door to Riverbank Outfitters.

Historic Kuebler - Waldrip Haus & Danville School

This Bed and Breakfast is situated on a peaceful 43 acre ranch that has two pioneer houses nestled on a scenic property. Both have been lovingly restored by the Waldrip family; Margaret and her three sons.

Upon your arrival you may be warmly greeted by the family dogs; Piggy and Rooster. Inside, you will find a couple of cats and perhaps a tame deer by the name of Baby Doll snoozing comfortably in a chair in the living room.

The main house was built in 1847, (The Waldrips' are the third family to live here since it was built) and is constructed of limestone and exposed timber. Family photos, pioneer memorabilia and artifacts from Mexico are throughout. Nine large bedrooms are decorated in a country setting with ceiling fans and four poster beds with quilts and comfy chairs. All have private baths and three have jacuzzis and kitchenettes. One of these rooms has a small deck that is a relaxing and private, spot for stargazing.

The Danville School House is a quaint, two story structure that was built in 1863 and has four rooms and five baths. The first floor has an authentic school room with chalkboard, teachers desk and private bedroom. A one-of-kind Romantic Rendezvous! There is also a private deck here and a new elevated shared deck that offers beautiful views of the area.

During the day, search out a secluded picnic spot on the property or enjoy croquette, volleyball or relaxing moments in front of the fireplace. At night, twinkling stars light up the country sky. In the morning, a hearty, country breakfast may include, super fluffy, fresh baked cinnamon rolls (baked by Margaret) and blueberries with cream. An adventure into the past, The serene setting of this B&B makes this a personal favourite.

Guestroom rates: $95.00 – $150.00
1620 Hueco Springs Loop • New Braunfels, Texas 78132
210.625.8372 ~ 800.299.8372

Gruene Country Homestead Inn

*H*ave you ever wondered what it would be like to reside on a country homestead? Gruene Country Homestead Inn offers you glimpses of the past preserved in a rustic setting.

Robert Fletcher

Ed and Billie Miles have maintained the historic theme of this estate by buying many old homes, moving them here, and then going through the arduous task of restoration. The setting is of country splendor seen only on television or in movies, (at the time of this authors visit, Ozarka Water was filming a commercial) and is accented by a windmill towering protectively over eight acres of land.

As you take in the surroundings, enjoy the transition from a Victorian home to a vintage farmhouse and then to a romantic cottage. Enter the 1905 Faust House through a glass breezeway to discover a relaxing living room, dining area and two guestrooms decorated in the elegance of the early 1900s; the Angel Room and the Garden Room.

The Cottage is attached to the Faust House and the 1859 Farmhouse includes the Judge's Chambers, Miss Lilli's Room, Oma's Suite and the Backroom. All are embellished with an unique decor that is guaranteed to delight all who visit. Scarlett's Room is an old root cellar that was used for storing veggies... and hiding from the Indians (in the 1800s)!

The Texas House (early 1900s) has two Texas size suites, The Yellow Rose Room is an ideal romantic getaway with a private sitting porch, the

Bluebonnet room exudes the pride of Texas with the colours and elegance of the state flower, that is painted throughout the room.

The Country House (early 1900s) has four suites that include The Attic which is decorated in soft pastel blue and a painted ceiling that reflects Texas skies. The back porch on this house allows for relaxing moments during your stay.

Enjoy the grounds and the manicured gardens, watch a beautiful sunset (or sunrise if you're up early) from your porch and then head back to your room for a romantic soak in a claw foot tub or whirlpool bath.

The recently completed Hanz Halle meeting chamber includes a commercial kitchen and will be able to accommodate 150 guests, ideal for retreats, weddings, receptions or corporate meetings. An onsite swimming pool with spa for relaxing moments in the country air.

A Continental breakfast is served on the wide, wrap around porch of the Victorian House, or in the elegant dining room. As you begin your day in these refreshing surroundings, enjoy the scenery and visions of yesteryear.

As you can imagine, this is a very unique place where unforgettable adventures to another time and place are yours to enjoy. Whatever room you choose, rest assured that your privacy is guaranteed and that your stay will be a relaxing excursion into the world of romance.

GRUENE COUNTRY HOMESTEAD INN
Guestroom rates: $95.00 – $125.00
832 Gruene Road • New Braunfels, Texas 78130 • 210.606.0216

Prince Solms Inn

*H*ere is a trip into the rich German heritage that was developing in many parts of Texas in the 1800's. Conveniently located on the Main Plaza, this Inn was built by German Craftsmen in 1898 and still emits an aura of European elegance and grace. Owner Deborah Redle, proud of her German heritage, has kept her family legacy alive by investing her love into this historic property.

Named after Prince Solms of Braunfels, Germany, this property has many other historic structures, including stables built soon after the city was established in 1845, a feed store constructed in 1860, and the Joseph Klein House that was built in 1852. You will find a picturesque courtyard in a shaded garden filled with beautiful plants and flowers. Notice the stones that were used for this area, imported from a prison that once stood in New Braunfels at the turn of the century. At night, relax around the outdoor fireplace for a very romantic interlude.

Accommodations include two suites on the ground floor and eight rooms upstairs. Each has a private bath, individualized decor and unique lamps and chandeliers. Many are named for the distinctive wallpaper in each room – the Rose, Magnolia, Peony, Songbird And Huntsman.

A Continental-plus breakfast is available for guests each morning. You can begin your day in the parlor, or in the courtyard to the sounds of chirping birds. After breakfast, enjoy the beautiful paintings throughout the inn.

There are Mystery Weekends in the Fall and Spring. "Romance Packages" (year round) include a bottle of champagne or sparkling cider, chocolates, turn down service, late check out time, and a gift certificate for fine dining.

For those searching for peace, relaxation and romance in a wonderful setting, you are sure to remember your visit to Prince Solms Inn.

PRINCE SOLMS INN
Guestroom rates: $85.00 – $150.00 - Dbl
295 E. San Antonio
New Braunfels, Texas • 78130
210.625.9169 ~ 800.625.9169

George Craig

Wolfgang's Keller Restaurant

Located down the stairs at the side of the Inn, this restaurant emits an unforgettable aura of romance. Tucked in a large brick basement in a setting that is reminiscent of a wine cellar, you will find intimate tables, soft candlelight and a cozy atmosphere. In the winter, a fireplace emits a warm sensual glow, while a musician sets the mood for intimate conversations.

After dinner, take a stroll through the area and then enjoy a satisfying night of sleep.

Historic Accommodations of Texas

295 E. San Antonio • New Braunfels, Texas 78130
800.625.9169 ~ 210.625.9169

Unusual adventures in the New Braunfels area include the Natural Bridge Caverns where you can tour caves with beautiful colours, translucent rocks and rooms the size of football fields. Extraordinary care went into the development of these caves and except for the lights and smooth walkways, you will see this underground wonder much as its discoverers did in 1960 ~ 210.651.6101. The Schlitterbahn Resort and Park has a wide selection of water slides to enjoy ~ 210.625.2351 and Circle-S Riding Stables takes you on guided tours through scenic countryside. ~ 210.629.9962. Or, how about an unforgettable camping excursion under the stars at Rainbow Campgrounds. ~ 210.964.2227.

Karbach Haus

*I*n this traditional B&B setting, guests experience the Gemütlichkeit of a German Gasthaus with the amenities of a romantic, upscale resort. Stately and casually elegant, the home boasts turn-of-the-century ambiance with twenty-first century comforts.

A world-class, multi-course breakfast is yours to savour each morning in the sun room or formal dining room. The gourmet delights are expertly prepared and graciously served by the owners/host, Kathy and Ben Jack Kinney.

Each spacious guest room has a private tiled bath, queen or king-size bed, cable TV/VCR, ceiling fan, down quilts, and many antiques and family heirlooms. The 18'x40' swimming pool and spa are set in beautiful landscaped gardens, surrounded by ancient pecan, cypress and magnolia trees.

Conveniently located on an acre estate in the heart of downtown New Braunfels, visitors may stroll to a superb variety of restaurants, museums, antique stores and recreational activities. Romance packages are available.

Guestroom rates: $100.00 ~ $200.00
487 West San Antonio Street • New Braunfels, Texas 78130
210.625.2131 ~ 800.972.5941

Finer Things B&B

Offering seclusion on a 50 acre country ranch, this property is near the north side of Canyon Lake and has magnificent vistas, hiking trails and private picnic spots. Although isolated from the rest of the world, Blanco and Johnson City are only minutes away.

Elegant rooms with private baths are furnished with antiques, collectibles and fine art. After a restful night of sleep, lovers of all ages are sure to appreciate the serenity of this property. Pat and Don Klesick offer guests a breakfast menu called "The Pleasure of the Guest" (as well as a high tea) which can be served on decks overlooking the vast hillsides.

• 210.833.2524 •

Kerrville

Located in the heart of the Hill Country, Kerrville offers an array of activities that might begin at the Tranquility Walk in the city park on Guadalupe Street. Follow this with a visit to the Hill Country Museum, a beautifully restored Victorian mansion, that portray the affluent life in the Hill Country's early days ~ 210.896.8633. Enjoy a stage production under the stars at The Point Theater ~ 210.367.5121, horseback riding at Lazy Hill Guest Ranch ~ 210.640.3222, Rodeos and Country Western Dancing on summer weekends ~ 210.792.3535, and the Kerrville Wine & Music Festival on Labor Day Weekend.

The true magic of Kerrville is its proximity to miles of country roads that inspire an afternoon or early evening drive. Pack a picnic basket and search out spots to pull over near sparkling spring fed creeks that meander through the rugged terrain and rolling hills of the Guadalupe River Valley.

Drive Northwest on 27 from Kerrville into a stunning rocky canyon, head West on 41 and discover rolling hills with forests and fields. This road seems to go on forever, (you may not encounter another car for 20 – 30 minutes) and during your travels you will see deer and elk feeding at Thompson Temple's Texas Wildlife. At the intersection of 1340 and 41 is Y.O. Ranch, a native and exotic game ranch that offers guided tours where you will see Zebras, Giraffes, Antelopes and 36 species of exotic game in open country ~ 210.640.3222.

Unforgettable memories begin when you turn right on 1340, a winding road that takes you along the Guadalupe River. Keep a sharp eye out for the gravel road that is just past Stowers Road (by the 55 M.P.H. sign) and you will find another great evening kissing spot. A few miles further is Rock Bottom Road, (about 100 hundred yards before the MO-Ranch sign) follow it and you will discover a low water bridge and a wonderful pullover spot ideal for stargazing.

When visiting Kerrville, consider a stay at the Holiday Inn – Y.O. Hilton Hotel. This expansive property is filled with Texas treasures and original Western art and an interesting lobby has many stuffed animals that include deer and elk, a gigantic bear and a giraffe with its baby (not to worry – this baby was stillborn). The rooms are very spacious and comfortable and a large swimming pool is the perfect place to get a Texas Tan ~ 800.531.2800. The River Run B&B is a classic, cut-stone and tin-roofed inn with six rooms ~ 800.460.7170, and the River Inn has one of the most romantic waterfronts around, complete with paddleboats, waterfalls and a lighted cliff at night. For an enjoyable dinner or lunch, dine at Annemarie's Alpine Lodge ~ 210.895.5000. For a great map of the area, call: 800.221.7958.

Fredericksburg

Easy accessibility to many Hill Country excursions is a plus, when you stay in this small bustling town, founded in 1846 by German settler. Over 250 inns grace Fredericksburg these days, testimony to its timeless and gentle appeal. Spectacular boutique shopping draw women from all over Texas.

A journey into the past is yours to enjoy any time of the day as you walk hand in hand through historic neighborhoods. Be sure to visit Grape Creek Vineyard and sample fine Texas wines (10 miles east on Hwy 290) and the Fredericksburg Herb Farm, an organic herb garden has rows of carefully tended flowers, antique roses and ornamental herbs that are harvested for gourmet vinegars, olive oils, seasonings, teas and other neat stuff ~ 402 Whitney.

Two unique dining experiences include; **The Plateau** in the heart of town, with an outdoor patio and twinkle lights in the trees, a perfect spot on a warm night. (the peppered Tenderloin with Amaretto Sauce is very good and a house favourite). **Hilltop Cafe**, 10 miles North on 87 is a fun restaurant in an old fashion country gas station that has a host of cool 50s and 60s memorabilia, a great 47' AMI Jukebox, and old blues and country western albums and posters on the walls. Owner John Nicholas, a former member of the band; Asleep at the Wheel, serves great tasting, healthy foods (presented in a creative down home fashion) such as Greek Special Tenderloin, Seafood Boudin, Crab Au Gratin and Frog Legs. A Sunday Champagne Brunch features Eggs Benedict and other delights. This is a great way to begin to your day. Average price per person: $10.00 – $20.00. Reservations recommended: 210.997.8522

Gästehaus Schmidt ~ B&B Reservation Service

With the wide variety of Bed & Breakfast establishments in Fredericksburg to choose from, why not use a reservation service to make your decision easier. A collection of over 100 properties includes traditional B&Bs and private guest houses, all unique in their own special way.

Established in 1985, this business has grown considerably over the years and is the largest quality referral service in town. Choose from Victorian to rock houses, log cabins and intimate Sunday Houses which were built by out of town farmers in order to have a place to stay when they came into town for the weekends.

When you call this reservation service you speak with a well-versed staff who will go out of there way to find exactly what you are looking for. If you are still undecided, a booklet listing many B&B's can be sent to you to peruse.

If you are in Fredericksburg and considering future lodging options, be sure to stop in at this establishment. Here you will be able to have one-on-one contact with the staff and review a wide assortment of photographs and information of the numerous properties available.

A few favourites B&B include Texas Two Step & A Little Waltz , Austin Street Retreat, Schildknecht-Weidfeller House, Das Kleine Nest, Schmidt Barn, Yellow House and Annie's Cabin.

Rates: Range from $60.00 ~ $125.00
231 West Main • Fredericksburg, Texas 78624 • 210.997.5612
Interent: http://www.ktc.com/GSchmidt ~ Email: gasthaus @ ktc.comm

MOONLIGHT PICNIC

At the intersection of 1340 and 39 outside of Kerrville, you will be amazed at the exact reproduction of Stonehenge, and Easter Island figureheads in an open field. This is a "Must Do" destination! Try a midnight picnic on the stone table or come to celebrate sunrise or moonrise. Afterwards, stop at the Tea House restaurant in Hunt for a nice break from the world in a simple, down home setting. 210.238.4484

Watkins Hill Bed and Breakfast

Unquestionably, the premier Bed and Breakfast in Fredericksburg. An atmosphere of peaceful charm radiates from this two-acre estate that includes four landscaped garden areas. A view of Barons Creek and green pastures with a small herd of Longhorn cattle grazing peacefully, is an inspiration for those seeking rest and relaxation.

Mr. Watkins takes great pride in sharing his 1855 pioneer stone residence with his guests. On weekends, you will receive a handwritten note inviting you to join him for drinks at his spectacular home, and a tour of the grounds. During the week, you are encouraged to discover the property in the afternoons.

Seven individual buildings include the 1855 pioneer house filled with fine 18th and 19th century antiques, an 1835 log house, a late 19th century rustic farm building and turn-of-the-century cottages. Nine of the eleven rooms and suites have fireplaces. All are decorated with antiques from the 1800s.

The newly completed main lodge is an awe-inspiring architectural adventure to another place and time. This expansive, two story building is built around an enormous 1840 hand-hewn timber barn which serves as a Frontier Ballroom and includes a parlor and library, both with fireplaces, a conservatory, and dining/board room. Upstairs are two multi-room suites and two large log rooms.

Amenities abound and all of the guestrooms have cathedral ceilings, canopy beds, TV and VCR, private telephone, beautiful linens, special travel cosmetics, soaps and bubble bath. Every room has its own porch, private bath with a garden tub or claw foot tub, and a Butler's pantry with bar, sink, and small refrigerator stocked with goodies. Snacks throughout the room and chocolates by your bed are special touches.

A full gourmet breakfast is brought to your door in a heart-shaped basket at a pre-arranged time. The menu changes on a daily basis and includes specialties such as quiche, German sausage rolls, soufflé, crepes, cakes and breads.

The professional staff can arrange whatever services you require, or if you desire, complete privacy for a romantic rendezvous. Is this a special occasion? If so, a silver champagne bucket is brought to your room on a silver tray with two flutes and a personal note of congratulations. By request, a romantic candlelight dinner can be served in your room. English-style wicker baskets are available by prior arrangement for romantic outings.

A gift shop on the property (for guests only) includes unique selections made by Mr. Watkins as well as a delightful display of collectibles from all over the world. A specially prepared "Directory of the Best Places to Dine" may inspire a romantic evening in town. This property is by far the best spot in Fredericksburg for special events, meeting, seminars and of course...beautiful weddings.

Located only one block from the Main Street shops, cafes and galleries, the feel of luxury and privacy in the country is yours to savour at this Inn. So enjoy a visit to a peaceful, gentler time among the hills. Your privacy is guaranteed!

Founding member: Historic Accommodations of Texas.

Guestroom rates: $100.00 ~ $225.00 ~ Average price: $122.00
608 East Creek • Fredericksburg, Texas 78624
800.899.1672 ~ 210.997.2154 ~ Fax: 210.997.2154

Enchanted Rock State Natural Area is 18 miles north of Fredericksburg on RR 965 and is a beautiful drive any time of the day. This scenic landscape is dominated by pink coloured granite and a massive dome-shaped rock. The view from the top of the dome is breathtaking, and the climb up is far less taxing than you'd first expect. You can enjoy hiking, climbing, backpacking and of course... Picnicking! 917.247.3603

A Little Waltz and The Texas Two Step

Owner Anne Weigers, in creating two of the most elegant guesthouses in Fredericksburg, has incorporated a blend of intimate and personal touches that are sure to win any romantic heart. These properties are adjacent to one another and offer a private, secluded retreat from the rest of the world. Lets begin with...

A LITTLE WALTZ

Enter through antique gates that lead into an enchanting courtyard with a New Orleans ambiance. The magnificent queen size, pencil post bed and feather comforter with lots of pillows... is very inviting. A fireplace next to the bed, wonderful art and antiques are the finishing touches to this very intimate setting. The bathroom has a tub for two, the skylight lets in the light of the morning sun and the evening moon and an abstract mural (painted by your hostess) surrounds the tub.

In the morning, enjoy a gourmet breakfast served on antique china in the elegant dining room, furnished with a French fruitwood table and English Yorkshire chairs, or in the enclosed sunroom with its a view of the beautiful outdoors.

THE TEXAS TWO STEP

If you appreciate the pleasure of romance, you are sure to enjoy this house. Your private entrance opens to a sun filled hallway between the bedroom and living room. Antique "twelve over twelve" windows offer soothing views of the outdoor patio. In the cozy living room you will find a fireplace made from local limestone and furnishings with marvelous New Orleans antiques. The bedroom features a cathedral ceiling with high windows, and the 1853 four poster Mallard bed has carved pineapples on each post.

The bathroom has a shower, tub for two and a large skylight. In the kitchen, you will find fixin's for a full breakfast of heart-shaped waffles, sausages, fruit and New Orleans Café au Lait. Enjoy your feast in the charming country kitchen, or on the outside patio.

Guestroom rates: $125.00 for two non-smoking adults
Reservations: 210.997.5612 @ Gästehaus Schmidt

San Antonio

Place me like a seal over your heart,
Like a seal on your arm;
For love is as strong as death,
Its jealousy unyielding as the grave.
It burns like a blazing fire,
Like a mighty flame.
Many waters cannot quench love;
Rivers cannot wash away

~ Song of Solomon 8:6,7

San Antonio

Rich in Texas history, San Antonio's main claim to fame is the Alamo, which isn't as big as you would expect (you'd think word would get around). For an interesting perspective of the city, enjoy a cocktail or dinner at the Tower of Americas. You can't miss it. It's the Space Needle-like structure with a revolving restaurant on top. The ride up the high speed elevator is a real rush and upon entering the restaurant, be prepared for stunning vistas, and sunsets, of San Antonio. 210.223.3101

The Riverwalk The Riverwalk is the major tourist draw in San Antonio. Here sidewalks accented with beautiful trees and native plants run along the San Antonio River, leading through a maze of quaint old buildings, restaurants, clubs and shops. This is a unique excursion while visiting and a fun adventure to share at night as you walk along the waters edge. Be careful! There aren't any guard rails on the river. At the beginning of the week in the late afternoon, the Riverwalk by the downtown section (daytime only) is a peaceful excursion. The flatboat tours are an interesting way to get a feel for the vicinity. If you're lucky enough to be in a sparsely populated boat, you may be able to organize a mutiny and convince your guide to stop talking and enjoy a quiet ride through the channels.

The Fiesta San Antonio is a yearly event that takes place at the end of April. This is a mini Mardi-Gras atmosphere and an assortment of events throughout the week include a street parade, concerts, Mariachi bands and whatnot. Christmas in San Antonio is extremely beautiful and begins with the lighting of the tree in Alamo Plaza. Immediately following is the River Walk Holiday Parade, where many boats in holiday regalia cruise down the river. More than 50,000 lights illuminate the bridges and trees above the parade watchers. Information: 210.824.1797.

Majestic Theater One of the few remaining vintage movie palaces of the 20's, this theater was restored in 1989. Here you can see many stage productions and the San Antonio Symphony throughout the year. The balcony seats offer an interesting perspective of the fine craftsmanship throughout. Stop in the bar during the course of a show and ask the bartender to turn the lights down low for a true Art Deco experience. 210.226.5700

La Mansion

This historic hotel is certainly one of San Antonio finest. The feel of a private hacienda is incorporated into 337 rooms decorated in a Spanish Colonial flavour with rough-hewn beamed ceilings, brick walls, traditional hand-finished furnishings, and soft contemporary colours. Along one side of the building, private balconies overlook the river. Terraces on the opposite side of the hotel look onto the swimming pool, sparkling fountains, quiet courtyards and lush landscaping.

Las Canaris, one of the River Walk's most elegant restaurants, promises an extraordinary dining experience for connoisseurs of fine foods. Although the indoor restaurant is very nice, the riverside veranda is magical on a warm evening. Favourite appetizers include the Trio of Grilled Venison Ravioli, Texas Escargot, Sweet Corn and Red Pepper Chowder, all of the salads are delicious. Entrees include Seven Spiced Fresh Tuna Steak, Roasted Pheasant Breast and Grilled North American Elk. For dessert, the Sweet Pumpkin and White Chocolate Mousse Cake is a true slice of heaven! After dinner, order a Press Coffee, prepared tableside. The Sunday brunch is the best in town and on opening nights of a new production or concert at the Majestic theater, a theater menu is offered before the show.
• Inquire about the Romance Packages

Guestroom rates: $99.00 – $280.00
Average price per person: $30.00 – $40.00
112 College Street • San Antonio, Texas 78205
800.292.7300

The Riverside Bayou ~ Of all the restaurants on the Riverwalk, this is a personal favourite. Relax on the outdoor cafe and people watch, or enjoy a romantic candlelight dinner by the picture windows on the second floor indoor restaurant (most romantic tables; 9 & 2). The waitstaff is very knowledgable and if you are unfamiliar with cajun foods, they will explain the dishes to you in great detail. Grandma Cace's Famous Shrimp Gumbo is a great appetizer, as is the Avocado Shrimp Remoulade salad. Excellent entrees include the Catfish fillet, the Shrimp Barataria and the New Orleans Barbecued Shrimp. Anything with the spicy barbecue sauce is a wonderful taste sensation. For dessert, the Baked Apple Pie is served in a hot skillet and topped with a Burgundy brandy sauce. Yummy!

Average price per person: $10.00 – $20.00
Located at the corner of College and North Presta Streets.
210.223.6403

Creative Chocolates Are you searching for that perfect gift for your sweetheart? Then this is the place for you! Owner Richard Berchin, a true romantic, specializes in custom chocolate designs and prides himself on being able to make anything and everything, in all sizes and shapes, out of chocolate. Unique creations include, dipped strawberries, flowers, gift boxes, champagne bottles and 3 dimensional objects. The store is a great place to browse and search for unique gift items. Custom orders are designed to fit any budget and one-of-a-kind chocolate creations are specialties of the house. A personal favourite of this author, Creative Chocolates is sure to win the heart of that special person in your life. And of course, everything can be delivered... Enjoy!
   999 East Basse Road, Suite 138 • San Antonio, Texas 78209 •
   210.824.2462

St. Anthony Hotel A beautiful hotel in the heart of downtown, the St. Anthony preserves and embodies the unique history and flavour of San Antonio in a modern, meticulously furnished facility. Located across from historic Travis park and next to the beautiful St. Mathews church, this hotel has a reputation for elegance and old world style. The grand lobby has many priceless museum-quality antiques and objects d'art throughout. Prominently displayed in the lobby is the famed painting "Monarch of the Golden West". 350 spacious guest rooms and 42 suites feature European furnishings and an elegant decor that is sure to delight the discriminating traveler. A rooftop pool is a pleasure to enjoy on a warm day.
   Guestroom rates: $120.00 $160.00
   300 East Texas • San Antonio, Texas 78205 • 800.227.6963

Victoria's Black Swan An unforgettable dining destination, discover the romance of Southern elegance when you visit this 1897 mansion in Solido Valley. As you enter the restaurant, it is like taking a trip back in time. Beautiful vistas of the surrounding country inspire thoughts of romance. A romantic setting is complemeted by candlelit tables, soft light from crystal chandeliers, and an intimate atmosphere. The menu changes daily and includes a pre planned five course meal. The Apple or Strawberry Romanoff and Chocolate truffle Mousse are exceptional desserts. After dining, take a walk on the property or enjoy the beautiful outdoor patio. For a special occasion, arrange for the horse drawn carriage to pick you up in front of the house for a ride in the country. This property is the ideal spot for a birthday, private party, luncheon, wedding or reception. The Sunday Brunch is a great way to finish off a romantic weekend!
   Pre fixe dinner price: $42.00 per person.
   1066 Holbrook • San Antonio, Texas 78218
   210.90.2507

Hyatt Hill Country Resort

Located in the scenic loop, this sprawling, full-scale resort is tucked away on 200 tree-covered acres on the northwestern outskirts of San Antonio in the Scenic Loop. As you enter the lobby with Southwest and country accents, you are sure to notice the majestic stone fireplace. This is a great place to sit and relax in comfy couches any time of the day. 500 spacious rooms and suites have stenciled trim on the walls and maple beds with washed pine finish and tall carved headboards. Most rooms feature French doors that open to wood-trimmed porches and scenic views.

Consider a "toobing" excursion down the 950 foot long man-made Ramblin' River that travels through a lushly landscaped, 4 acre park patterned after area rivers. An 18 hole golf course, tennis courts and health club with jacuzzi and sauna are available for all guests. After a restful day, enjoy dinner at Antlers Lodge, a full service restaurant specializing in Southwestern cuisine. High ceilings, a large stone fireplace and antler chandeliers make this an interesting dining experience. After dinner, cuddle by the fireplace in the outdoor covered pavilion and then search out kissing spots along the many pathways.

Guestroom rates: $190.00 – $230.00
9800 Hyatt Regency Dr. • San Antonio, Texas, 78205
210.647.1234

Grey Moss Inn ~ While in the Scenic Loop, visit this restaurant that serves fine foods in an intimate atmosphere. Built in 1929, it is situated near a wildlife sanctuary where you may see native white tailed-deer grazing in the nearby meadow. Majestic oaks paint a picture perfect setting for romance. Average price per person: $17.00 – $35.00. 210.695.8301

King Williams District This picturesque area reflects the history of the San Antonio. While touring this area you will see block after block of homes that look like they belong on old-fashioned engravings or movie sets. Gingerbread mansions, cut-limestone cottages with tin roofs and a variety of other architectural designs are sure to delight the senses. There are numerous B&B's in this area guaranteed to appeal to those with discriminating taste. Drive, walk or bike the streets in search of interesting B&Bs and when you see one that sparks an interest, retrieve a brochure from the front of the house, or ask for a tour (best times: 1:00pm – 3:00pm).

Noble Inns

Another fine choice in the heart of the King William Historic District, the Noble Inns consist of two, luxury Victorian Bed & Breakfast properties. Both are meticulously restored and furnished with attention to detail with Victorian antiques, reproduction wallpapers and coordinated, custom-made window coverings and bed ensembles.

Owners, Donald Pancoast Noble and Liesl Macdaniel Noble are San Antonio natives and descendants of King William founding families. Consequently, when they walk through this neighborhood on a warm summer night, they feel as if they are walking through a family album.

The Jackson House is a traditional B&B with six rooms in an 1894 home. Savour relaxing moments on the native-limestone patio while soaking up the Texas sun in a chaise lounge, or take a dip in the 14 ft. heated swim-spa located in the conservatory with 19th century, English stained glass windows. A full breakfast is served in the dining room and includes a main entree, fruit, home-made breads or muffins, cereals and yogurt. An exercise room is equipped with a rowing machine. exercycle and other equipment.

Pancoast Carriage House, built in 1896, is a suite arrangement and features three suites. A private, fenced brick patio overlooks a garden with a swimming pool and heated spa and an additional patio with chaise lounges, table and chairs. A relaxing, continental breakfast is provided in the kitchen of each suite for guests to enjoy at their leisure.

Luxurious, private marble baths are found in all nine room arrangements, some boast two-person Jacuzzi bathtubs. Gas fireplaces with antique mantels add that special touch, guaranteed to win your heart. For those visiting Noble Inns, this is your opportunity to discover the beautiful architecture and Victorian splendor of this historic part of town at your leisure.

Guestroom rates: $105.00 ~ $135.00
102 Turner Street • San Antonio, Texas 78204
210.224-7300 ~ 800.221.4045 Fax: 210.979.6825

First Dates And Inexpensive Dating Tips

Many people aren't sure how they feel about someone until the second or third date. Here are a few low-budget options that enable two people to discover if they have something in common.

Brunch works well as a neutral and pleasant beginning. On first dates, consider coffee, cappuccino, espresso or juice, opposed to liquor (if the chemistry is there, you won't need liquor). Going out for dinner does not mean spending a lot. Many restaurants offer early bird specials, a variety of reasonably priced appetizers and a selection of inexpensive wine. Appetizers and a basket of bread can take an introduction a long way.

The perfect or near-perfect date can be enhanced by doing a little research. Check out the places ahead of time to see if it's the atmosphere you are looking for and if it fits in your price range. Look for hidden, unique and unusual places, and if possible, be prepared to have a few other options tucked away in your mind.

Monte Vista

A unique neighborhood with mnay of historic homes and mansions, this charming area is an undiscovered section of San Antonio that is sure to win your heart. Upon further exploration, you will discover that this part of town is less opulent and certainly more reserved than the King Williams District. Sadly, the San Antonio tourist guides rarely touch on this district, located within the approximate boundaries of San Pedro, E. Hildebrand, Shock and W. Ashby Streets. Whether you drive, bike or walk, you are sure to enjoy this adventure into the past. Here, beautiful buildings with intricate architectural designs blend with elegant masonry creations and tree-shaded landscaped lawns. A quiet evening walk is a magical step back in time.

You can lunch at Magnolia Gardens which has an upstairs balcony with intimate tables overlooking the main dining area below. Next door is a great gift shop that has a variety of unusual and unique items guaranteed to please that hard-to-shop-for partner. Other favourite restaurants include Chez Ardid which serves fine French Cuisine, Biga's specializes in wild game, Paesano, Italian food at it's finest, and Banana Billiards, a casual setting where you can have good steaks and then play a game of billiards. Bed & Breakfast establishments include, The Academy House, Adelynne's Summit Haus, The Belle of Monte Vista, Brookhaven Manor, O'Casey's and the Victorian Lady. Call Brookhaven Manor for more information: 210.733.3939.

O'Caseys Bed And Breakfast

A quiet and informal Bed and Breakfast with a lot of character, the Irish theme is enhanced by the presence of owners John and Linda O'Casey. Located in the Monte Vista Historic District and surrounded by turn of the century homes, the prominent features of this 1904, two-story house are its stately columns and spacious wrap-around porch and balcony.

When you enter the large foyer, you will see edge-gain pine floors and the staircase, cozy living room and dining areas. The decor is designed with comfort in mind in an informal atmosphere of spacious surroundings.

Four rooms with private baths include the Master Bedroom which is furnished with an antique wardrobe, dresser and secretary desk; it has access to the front balcony. A large private bath has an old claw foot tub with polished brass fixtures. The East Suite opens onto the front balcony and has a queen size bed and a triple dresser. There is a platform bathroom (one step up!) with an old-fashioned tub. The North Suite is a friendly pair of rooms that are decorated with a taste of the Southwest and a park bench, an Indian design rug and a clawfoot tub. The Downstairs Bedroom is furnished with two full beds and is ideal for a small family.

A Continental-plus breakfast is served at your convenience and includes a variety of treats to begin your day.

After you have spent a day exploring the quiet residential neighborhood, relax a moment and enjoy refreshing breezes on either of the outdoor patios. Your home away from home, O'Caseys is a pleasant Bed and Breakfast that emits down-home Texas hospitality.

O'CASEY'S
Bed & Breakfast

Guestroom rates: $60.00 ~ $90.00 • A smoke-free establishment
225 West Craig Place • San Antonio, Texas 78212
800.738.1378

Brookhaven Manor

An elegant, three-story Victorian home built in 1913, this B&B has high beam ceilings, hardwood floors and original fireplaces. Situated in the historic Monte Vista district, Brookhaven Manor is just minutes from many of San Antonio's most celebrated attractions including the Riverwalk, the Alamo, and the King Williams district.

Upon entering this B&B you will walk into a spacious living room, decorated with an assortment of antiques. A beautiful Mahogany staircase and baby grand piano make this a very picturesque setting. This portion of the house can be an inspirational spot for those who enjoy restful moments, lazy afternoons and evenings, or you can play one of the many board games available for guests. In the morning, a full breakfast is served in the elegant dining room and may include Blueberry and cream cheese French Toast, fruit, salad, muffins and cocktail sausage with juice and gourmet coffee.

Four spacious guestrooms have private baths and TV. The Murphy Room is cozy with an antique bureau, desk and a queen-size Murphy Bed, Rose Room has a Victorian theme, queen-size brass bed and mahogany furniture, Gallery Room is a spacious room with a private sitting room, there is a loveseat and a trundle bed, the Honeymoon Suite is an elegant room, reminiscent of a French country cottage. The king-size bed is decorated in black, tan and gold. This sanctum offers a private dressing room that has an adjoining marble bathroom with an antique claw-foot tub.

Are you in the mood for a picnic? The front yard of Brookhaven Manor has giant trees that provide an ample amount of shade. With a slight breeze rustling the leaves, this is a romantic setting indeed. As your day winds down, relax on the front porch and enjoy the historic splendor that this house has to offer.

Guestroom rates: $75.00 ~ $110.00
128 West Mistletoe • San Antonio, Texas 78212
210.733.3939 ~ 800.851.3666 ~ Fax: 210.733.3884

Bonner Garden Bed & Breakfast

Bonner Garden - a magnificent two-story Italian Villa, is surrounded by lush gardens, a large swimming pool, stone walls, and a wrought iron fence. It was built in 1910 by Mrs. CA. Bonner. Her daughter Mary, who became an internationally known artist, worked closely with Atlee B. Ayers, noted Architect, to lend her artistic influence to the home. The home is a replica of a Renaissance villa built in the early 1600s and is decorated with an array of Italian tiles, fireplaces, beautiful fixtures, ceramic works and paintings.

Mary spent much of her life in Paris where she captivated the city with her Texas-motif etchings and print-making skills. She returned to spend her last years in San Antonio to enjoy the home she loved. She died in 1935 at the age of 48, and left a rich heritage of art for the world to enjoy.

Five guest accommodations include King and Queen beds, private baths, TV, VCR and telephones. Three of these rooms have fireplaces and two have Jacuzzi bathtubs. Each morning breakfast is served in the intimate dining room. Guests can browse in the Texana library, relax by the pool or enjoy a movie from the VCR library. In the evening, enjoy star filled skies while relaxing on the roof-top-patio that overlooks San Antonio. An ideal location for a Romantic Rendezvous, take a step into the past and experience the beauty and tranquility of the early 1900s.

Guestroom rates: $75.00 ~ $125.00. Corporate rates available.
145 East Agarita • San Antonio, Texas 78212
210.733.4222 ~ 800.396.4222 ~ Fax: 210.733.6129
Internet: noels@onr.com

Red Roof Inn

~ An affordable alternative for those on a tight budget, Red Roof Inn is near the airport and only fifteen minutes from downtown San Antonio. National expansion has given these inns a reputation for quality and service in new buildings with the familiar red roof. Economical and comfortable, all rooms have telephones, remote control cable television with Showtime, ESPN and CNN, private bath and a pleasing decor. Coffee is served in the lobby in the morning and some inns allow pets.

Guestroom rates: $49.00 – $61.00
333 Wolfe Road • San Antonio • 800.843.7663

Driving In Texas.

Coming from a city where fearless drivers stake their lives on a ten foot break in traffic, driving the backroads of Texas was nothing short of a pleasure. The drivers are friendly and courteous, and often wave to you as they pass from the opposite direction. And of course, flashing headlights mean there is a police cars ahead.

Although the country roads are only two lanes, there is an additional lane on each side sectioned off by a white line. When you want to pass, it is common procedure for the driver ahead of you to pull over and let you pass. And of course, follow your maneuver with a wave.

Country drives allow for a romantic excursion in search of a picnic spot, especially during Springtime when colourful wildflowers line the roadsides. Or, make a reservation at a Bed & Breakfast and stop at the many small towns along the way. Bring a camera and search out the unique architecture of each town hall and compile a photo journal of your trip.

During your journey, you will see an occasional abandoned house in the middle of nowhere. These structures allow for good photo opportunities, a scenic picnic and quite possibly, a Romantic Rendezvous.

Highway signs with the Texas star and outline keep you on your course and cleverly worded anti-littering signs get the point across. Flowers and/or markers on the roadside point out the spot where a loved one lost their lives in an auto accident. This is a very sobering sight and an inspiration to slow down.

Once you arrive at your destination point, inquire about local scenic drives. And if you see an interesting side road, take a chance and explore. You may find many secluded picnic spots at your disposal. If you get lost, don't worry. Pull over at the first house you see, tell them you are lost, and ask for directions. You are probably only minutes away from a main road.

Romantic America Mail Order

Romantic Santa Barbara	$9.95
Romantic Big Bear	$9.95
The Romantic California Riviera and Catalina Island	$9.95
The Great Stays of Texas	$9.95
Romantic San Diego IV	$12.95
Romantic Southern California	$12.95
Romantic Texas	$12.95

Coming in 1997
Romantic California & The Romantic Southwest

♥ ♥ ♥

Are you searching for the perfect gift to share with your sweetheart? These unique games are guaranteed to put a spark in your relationship. Play them by candlelight with romantic music and strawberries soaking in champagne for an unforgettable *Romantic Rendezvous*.

An Enchanting Evening™ ~ This game is perfect for two people who want to share a sensual Fantasy Desire. Have fun finding out what really turns each other on and enjoy unforgettable memories. $25.00

Romantic Sensations™ ~ A card game that combines and reinforces the sense of Touch, Taste, Scent, Sound, and Sight and creates an unforgettable romantic experience for a couple. $22.00

♥ ♥ ♥

Do you have a favourite restaurant, B&B, place or romantic tip that you would like to share with us? Call or write our office and if we use your suggestion, we will send you a free *Romantic America* gift packet.

The Romantic America Internet site will be on-line in February 1997. Call our toll-free number for the URL, and/or for inclusion information

Receive a 10% discount when ordering direct
1.800.442.4815
4178 Sorrento Valley Blvd. Suite I • San Diego, Ca 92121

♥ • ♥ • ♥ • ♥ • ♥ • ♥ • ♥ • ♥ • ♥ • ♥

Love Note...

The Perfect Romantic Gift
Have you written a poem that you feel could be turned into a beautiful song? Pat Calloway is a proficient musician and specializes in doing just that! Send him your poem and he will compose a song using your lyrics. Rest assured that this individualized song will win the heart of that special person in your life. Majestic Records ~ 903.756.7696

Wildflower Country

To Birdie
The giver of this when he gave it
Was a man whom you didn't well know
But time has wrought many changes
And it seems now, like a tale that's been told
You didn't know then, that I loved you
But now, you know it is true.
For I have repeatedly told you
And still, the old story, seems new.

But now our hearts are united
And along life's path may we trend,
With one others care now upon us
Our darling, whose name we've not said

May our love in the future grow stronger
And our pathway be strewn with sweet flowers
Never forgetting the giver,
Who gave us, the love we call ours.

Written by Albion Rheiner Chew for his wife Birdie
Please see Albion Bed & Breakfast review

Lockhart

Lockhart is located 30 miles from Austin, and 20 miles from San Marcos. One can stroll the town square and admire its magnificent Courthouse as Lockhart is the county seat of Calwell County. The Dr. Eugene Clark Library, contains beautiful architecture and is the oldest continuously circulating library in the state of Texas.
Lockhart is known for Bar-B-Que and you can visit many local barbecue restaurants, get an order to go, and lunch in the cozy tree filled state park. The many antique stores are housed in beautiful historic buildings and offer a fine afternoon of exploration.? China Palace serves great Chinese food at reasonable prices ~ 512.398.999

Gonzales

Established in 1825, earned its place as the "Lexington of Texas" in 1835 when the first shot for Texas Independence was said to have been fired here by the "Come And Get It" canon, now displayed in the Memorial Museum. The Courthouse in the town square is a stunning display of Romanesque Revival architecture and the Old Jail Museum, built in 1887, is an interesting excursion. Many turn-of-the century homes (or older) are in the area – an inspiration to an afternoon drive or walk through old neighborhoods.
An assortment of antique and specialty shops in the downtown area are fun to explore and the Domino Bar, in operation before the turn-of-the-century, hasn't changed a bit! The Crystal Theater has live dinner performances and Accolade Restaurant, a former hotel, serves breakfast and lunch at reasonable prices. In the 1930s, Bonnie and Clyde once stayed here, and with the law hot on their trail, they jumped from a second story window to continue on their infamous tour of the South.
From majestic buildings to flowered fields, the rural attitude of this community is a refreshing sensation. It is this authors contention that Gonzales will experience a rebirth in the upcoming years and become a major destination point for Texans. Consequently, this is a great time to discover this historical town Chamber of Commerce: 210.672.6532

Albion Bed & Breakfast

Southern romance emanates at this beautiful 98 year old home, lovingly restored to its turn-of-the-century charm. An eclectic neo-classical, two story home with wrap around porches on both floors, a history of romance began with the construction of this house by Albion Rheiner Chew in 1898 and prevails to this day with the loving inspiration of owners Wendy and Ray Ramsey.

A poem written by Albion for his wife Birdie is reproduced in the beginning of this chapter. This poem reflects the love he felt for his wife. The five guestrooms are named for their children. Personal family memorabilia fills the house, including original antique pieces in the library and the bedrooms.

Each bedroom has a private bathroom and claw foot tub, queen-size beds with an extra feather mattress, down comforters and pillows, and many antiques. Albion and Birdie's Room represents the love this couple shared and has porch access and a fireplace. Rheiner's Room has a beautiful iron bed and a crochet hammock hangs in the barrel glass window, perfect for reading and smooching. Harry and Mamie's Room has a private balcony accessible only by sneaking out the window — a very romantic escapade for those with a youthful outlook on life.

Breakfast is served on beautiful mix-and-match antique dishes and includes everything from "heart healthy" to traditional Southern fare. Happy hour is served in the late afternoon and a night time snack of small sandwiches and hot chocolate await the guests upon their return in the evening. The grounds of this B&B have old fashioned roses, an English flower garden and the original brick pathway is lined with breathtaking day lilies. All of these areas are great Kissing Spots at night.

Wendy and Ray are true romantics and they delight in sharing their special touches and stories with their guests – an inspiration to all who visit.

Guestroom rates: $90.00 ~ $95.00
605 West San Antonio Street • Lockhart, Texas 78644
512.376.6775

The Houston House

A personal favourite, this B&B is a delightful surprise just 65 minutes from San Antonio! As you approach this unique house owned by Gene and Diana Smith, you will see a vintage automobile sitting elegantly in the driveway. Your thoughts are sure to drift to a different time and place.

Built in 1895 by William Buckner Houston, a noted Texas trail driver, this late Queen Anne Victorian home features towers, turrents, wraparound porches and other intricate embellishments.

Upon entering the arched entranceway, you will see a gorgeous formal staircase leading to the second floor. Take a quick peek into the living room to discover a beautiful hand painted ceiling mural of frolicking cherubs with garlands of roses. In the dining room, additional murals include European countrysides depicting a serene and gracious time. These paintings were painstakingly executed by Mr. Houston's wife Sue who studied art in Europe. Be sure to inspect them indepth during the course of your stay.

The Houston House is beautifully furnished with fine antiques, many dating as early as 1835. An impressive collection of over 35 clocks decorate the walls. Floral arrangements, potpourri and fine accessories accent each room, lending an air of romance and charm at every turn.

Four rooms offer guests a trip back into time. The Eastlake Room has a private bath and a massive sleigh bed with matching marble-topped washstand and dresser, and a magnificent 1840 wardrobe. You can relax in front of your private fireplace for a very romantic experience. Ada's Playroom is named after the Houston's daughter and displays an array of antique toys. A hand-carved blanket chest sits in front of a queen size four poster bed. The Emerald Room has eloquently arranged Victorian pieces that include a marble-top dresser and a Prudent mallard gentleman's armoir. The fireplace and decor are just a part of this cozy setting. The Estate Room is a true pleasure and features an 1860 Mallard half-tester bed (the hand-carved canopy is stunning!) with matching armoir and dresser. The true magic of this room is the high-back slipper clawfoot tub elegantly displayed in the attached tower room with a draped entryway. This room emits an aura of romance rarely found in today's bustling society.

In the morning, a full breakfast may include apple or cherry Bavarian pancakes or cinnamon raisin French toast with real Maple syrup. Bacon or sausage links and a fresh fruit smoothie are finishing touches to your first meal of the day.

As you can tell, this Bed and Breakfast is a one-of-a-kind experience accented by many personal touches. Gene and Diana go out of there way to make sure your stay continually brings you pleasant memories. On the weekend, if Gene is not busy, he will be happy to take you on a guided tour of Gonzales in an antique car. A true trip into the past.

The Houston House
Guestroom rates: $75.00 – $120.00
621 George Street • Gonzales, Texas 78629
210.672.6940

THINGS TO DO IN GONZALES
Discover treasure after treasure at Laurel Ridge Antiques and Christmas Corner where it is Christmas year-round! Wreaths, trees, specially blended potpourri, an exclusively designed Father Christmas, unique gift items and fine antique furnishings from American Classical to American Victorian are also on display. Your eyes will sparkle as you discover this beautiful store. 210.672.2484
A trip into the past begins with a visit to the Pioneer Village Living History Center. Here you will find a collection of restored 19th century homes and buildings in a setting that resembles an early Texas settlement. At the beginning of May, the Dutch Oven Cookout is a fun excursion. A number of events throughout the year include period demonstrations and historic reenactments. Don't forget to visit Uncle Billy's Petting Farm! ~ 210.672.2157

Round Top

Certainly one of the most unique small towns in Texas, Round Top, (population: 81), has many unexpected surprises. Let's discover them together...

Hinkle Square is an historic town square with antique shops and restaurants, The Sweet Tooth is a co-op that sells antiques, local artisans crafts and hand made candy, Round Top Visitors Center has an extensive collection of area history, and the Bethlehem Lutheran Church, built in 1866, has a hand-built 1867 pipe organ that is still in use. In back, a small cemetery has many headstones dating from the mid-1800s.

A visit to the renowned Winedale Historic Centre is a must! This complex of restored historic structures is dedicated to the study of ethnic cultures in central Texas. Tour the beautiful barn that has first-class theatrical performances, including Shakespearean Festivals and classical concerts. The interior has intricate workmanship and hand-crafted wood throughout. Afterwards, explore the area and discover a nature trail and picnic area.

A biannual antique event is held on first weekend of April and October. Thousands of "Antiqualopes" (see page 12) converge on this quiet little town in search of antique bargains. Be sure to book a place to stay well in advance. Lodging options include; Heart Of My Heart Ranch B&B, an expansive property with a beautiful Victorian home and a wrap-around porch that overlooks a forest and lake ~ 800.327.1242. Trickle Creek B&B is another adventure into the great outdoors and offers intimate accommodations in a scenic country setting ~ 409.249.3060.

Hungry? Be sure to enjoy lunch or a romantic dinner at the Round Top Cafe. Owner Bud Royer provides a first class menu (with a touch of humor) that offers excellent pasta dishes, sandwiches, soups and salads, "Things That Churped"; grilled and stuffed quail, grilled or lemon dipped chicken chest, chicken fried steak, "Things That Mooed And Oinked"; ribs, beef tenderloin, pork chops, and... PIES! PIES! PIES! All served fresh and with BBHV (Blue Bell Homemade Vanilla). Please note: there is a 5¢ service charge for pies served without BBHV. Shipped pies are not served with BBHV! 1.800.624.PIES

Briarfield at Round Top

About 3 miles from downtown Round Top on FM 954 sits a two story yellow "Sunday House" built in 1886 that is sure to catch your eye. This tin-roof house is nestled in a grove of trees on a sprawling five acre property with a split-rail fence.

Owners Roland Nester and his sister, Mary Nester Stanhope have created a cozy setting that is sure to win your heart. Five guestrooms are in the restored farmhouse and all have central air and heating, ceiling fans and private baths. The decor is accented by colourful quilts, painted hardwood floors, antique accessories, multi-paned windows, and custom handmade furniture created by Round Top master craftsmen. Favourite rooms include the Garden Room which gives the sensation of being in an outdoor garden, the Texas Room is decorated with old Texas maps, leather rugs and long horns, and the Americana Room has a Patriotic theme, prints of the American Revolution and an American Flag made of tin. The two-story cottage has an upstairs bedroom and living room and a bathroom and kitchen downstairs. Wingback chairs, colourful prints, a sleeper sofa and a private front porch and deck contribute to this relaxing setting.

Explore the grounds and discover rolling landscapes, stone walkways, chairs under shade trees, and rocking chairs and cedar post furniture on the porches and decks. A colorful garden is highlighted by a Lily pond and the sounds of chirping birds.

In the morning, the famous BasketBreakfast is delivered to your room at the requested time and features a warm continental-plus meal consisting of juice, fresh rolls, homemade muffins, kolaches and other tempting goodies

At Briarfield B&B, feelings of peace and serenity surround you when you are under the crystal-clear night skies. Wonderful displays of stars uncluttered by city lights and pollution are an inspiration to moonlit strolls and a Romantic Rendezvous. Enjoy!

BRIARFIELD AT ROUND TOP
Guestroom rates: Start at $75.00 per night, double occupancy.
219 FM 954 • Round Top, Texas 78954
409.249.3973 ~ Fax: 800.472.1134

The Settlement House

Catering to romance in beautiful country surroundings, The Settlement House provides a variety of historic lodging options in and around Round Top. Owners Karen and Larry Beevers have gone to great lengths to ensure that your stay is truly unforgettable and encourage visiting adults to enjoy the comforts of today, combined with the charms of yesteryear.

This unique Bed and Breakfast has seven guest rooms contained in four historic Texas houses, all with private baths, individual heat and air conditioning and porches with rockers.

The Town Place (Stadt Platz) is a combination of two restored 1880s Italian Renaissance farm houses and is located four blocks from the town square. Inside you will find a quaint county store and three charming guestrooms. The Cowboy Room is decorated with an impressive array of old west memorabilia and features a tin bath tub and an antique brass queen size bed with a down comforter to snuggle under. The Country Room has a queen size sleigh bed, country antiques and a cheery sunflower tiled shower, The Garden Room has two antique iron double beds and a spring garden decor. This room includes a marvelous bathroom with stained glass windows above an old claw foot tub that may inspire a candlelight rendezvous.

The shining light of this property is the back porch with ceiling fans. Here you can relax in comfort any time of the day and enjoy the picturesque

102 · Romantic Texas

countryside with views of towering oaks, a delightful picket fence and a small pond. Nearby is a small grove of trees perfect for a secluded picnic.

The Country Place, where your hosts reside, is a restored home built during the Civil War located on the edge of town on 35 acres of land. Three distinct, and private lodging accommodations include:

The Log Cabin, (Das Blockhaus) an 1830s two story cabin constructed of huge oak logs. The first floor has a buffalo hide rug covering a hand cut cedar floor, clawfoot tub and a stone fireplace that is sure to be an inspiration on a chilly night. Climb the cedar stairway into the cozy sleeping room (with hand hewn rafters and wood floor) to find a hand made 1830s double feather bed covered in Indian blankets and down comforters. The Little Nest (Das Kleine Nest) is a delightful 1869 cedar cottage ready to fulfill your countryside dreams. Completely furnished in period antiques, you will rest peacefully nestled on pillows and down comforters after a soothing bath in the huge claw foot tub. Cozy up to the old parlor stove and warm yourself on a cold winter night. The Sante Fe House is a late 1800s railroad depot with five large windows, an expansive porch ideal for bird watching, and a queen size bed surrounded by the images and lore of old Sante Fe.

In the morning, a full country breakfast is served in a picnic basket and brought to your door at a prearranged time. Fresh made breads, fruits, juices, fresh ground coffee and other delectable delights make this the perfect way to begin your day.

Ideal for an anniversary or surprise, all of the rooms at The Settlement House provide a haven from the outside world and many peaceful moments are guaranteed. Enjoy!

Guestroom rates: $90.00 ~ 180.00
Box 176 • Round Top, Texas 78954
409.249.5015 ~ 888 ROUND TOP (Toll free) Fax: 409.249.5015

The Round Top Register, is a lighthearted local publication produced by Christopher K. Travis. This newspaper is far from the standard norm of small town newspapers geared towards tourists. Students of National Lampoon or Mad Magazine are sure to enjoy such stories as; "Local Brewery Stormed By Excited Merchants", "Donkey-Headed Man Has Affair With Queen", "Register Locked In Print War With N.Y. Times", "Mayors Office Ruled By Political Dynasty", etc. Read these stories to your partner and many laughs are guaranteed! Yearly subscriptions: $5.00 ~ 409.249.5550.

Brenham

Home to Bluebonnets and Blue Bell Ice Cream, Brenham is situated in the heart of Washington County. Recognized as "The Birthplace of Texas", downtown Brenham has a quaint historical district with a variety of shops and restaurants. Must Be Heaven is an 1950s restaurant/soda parlor that deserves to be on your agenda. Check out the assorted memorabilia, drop some quarters in the Juke Box and enjoy a lunch of soup or sandwiches. Top off your experience with a shake, malt, phosphate soda, homemade pie or hand-dipped ice cream.

Fun excursions in town include a tour of the Blue Bell Creameries, followed by a visit to the eight acre retail display garden at the Antique Rose Emporium. Romantic old garden roses, native plants and other flowers can be purchased here. Several restored buildings are on this eight-acre property, and a wildflower meadow is the perfect backdrop for a garden weddings and reception. While on the subject of flowers, stop at Ellison's Greenhouses where you will find five, half-acre greenhouses chock full of mums, gloxinias, African violets and kalanchoes. A breathtaking walk through these structures is yours when seasonal flowers such as poinsettias, tulips and Easter Lilies are in bloom. The Brenham Downtown Association has a comprehensive brochure on the area: 409.830.8445

☆ Lone Star Rendezvous ✲✲✲

Brenham is close to a number of rural towns and unique attractions. A memorable afternoon drive through eye-appealing topography can begin on 290 East to Chappell Hill. Explore the Chappell Hill Historic District and take in the stunning antebellum structures and houses. Continue on 1155 to 17 to the town of Washington and search out Washington-on-the-Brazos Historical Park. This is a beautiful park with many choice picnic spots. Head Southwest on 105 towards Brenham and visit the Monastery of St. Clare home to a group of Franciscan Poor Clare Nuns who support themselves by raising Miniature Horses and selling handmade ceramic items in "The Art Barn". And yes.. you can pet the horses!

Ant Street Inn

A trip to Brenham wouldn't be complete unless you discover the Ant Street Inn located in the historic downtown district. As you approach this large mercantile building built in 1899, your first thoughts are of a curious nature until you pass through the large entranceway, where immediate thoughts of exploration enter your mind.

The spacious reception and event room has a beautiful stained glass chandelier and the dining room where an artfully arranged breakfast is served in the morning, has an antique wood bar and a stunning stained glass dome chandelier. This is the ideal place to enjoy quality time with your sweetheart any time of the day.

Fourteen luxury guest rooms are named after Southern towns and all have twelve foot ceilings, exposed brick walls, stained glass, polished wood floors and private baths. The Charleston is a romantic setting with a Rosewood queen bed and a bathtub for two, the Memphis Room features Gothic decor and a 100 year old freight elevator, (which may be an inspiration to a fantasy) and the Galveston is a 750 sq. ft. room with a sitting area, desk, game table, tub for two and a draped canopy queen bed with a magnificent carved footboard.

Owners Tommy and Pam Traylor traveled throughout the U.S. in search of 19th century American Antiques that have been incorporated into the decor. Comical accessories add a touch of whimsey and include old family photos, an umbrella lamp and a dentists chair. The real discovery is the red velvet Bourne in the first floor hallway. Built in 1870, this 8 ft. tall loveseat (which may have come from a bordello) has Egyptian Sphinx arm rests and is accented by a curved bonnet ~ a perfect Kissing Spot at night.

Relax in rocking chairs on the back balcony overlooking the courtyard, or explore the antique shops, enjoy Blue Bell Ice Cream (made locally) as a bed time snack, or sip a glass of wine or a chilled mug of micro-brewery beer in the smoke-free bar. However you choose to spend your day, this glorious self-indulgent B&B is sure to supply you with unforgettable memories for years to come.

Guestroom rates: $85.00 ~ $160.00
107 West Commerce • Brenham, Texas 77833
800.481.1951 ~ 409.836.7393 ~ Fax: 409.836.7595

Far View

If you have ever wondered what it would be like to savour the elegance of the Great Gatsby era, this is your opportunity to do so. Your mind's eye is sure to take you back in time as you approach this stately, two-story brick mansion built in 1925. Situated grandly on the crest of a hill, it boasts a panoramic view.

As you pass through the arched entry way, you will be drawn to the cozy library with a fireplace. A warm aura is highlighted by the handcrafted Grecian colonnade and fine old rugs that cover the white oak and longleaf pine floors. Fine touches such as period wallpaper, crystal doorknobs, and porcelain plumbing prove that this restoration by owners David and Tonya Meyer, was a true labor of love.

Five bedrooms include the intimate Hasskarl Room, which has a queen size bed, full private bath and views of huge oak trees. The rustic setting of the Star Room has a king size bed, private bath and is surrounded by pine trees. The Balcony Room has a Victorian decor, queen size bed and a clawfoot tub that looks out into the room. Access to the upstairs balcony makes this a very nice place to watch the stars at night. The Blue Room has a private bath and features a white iron king size bed in a relaxing setting that overlooks the garden. The Garden room is an elegant room with private bath.

Your day will begin with an elegant breakfast served in the Chippendale dining room. As the sun streams in through six stained glass windows, take this moment to survey the glistening chandelier above.

Exploring this property is sure to be a highlight of your day. Discover stained glass double sliding windows on the stair landing, Grecian urns on the lower porch, stunning views from the upper balcony, and a carriage house that was also built in 1925. Garden areas with table and chairs is the perfect spot to sip iced tea or take a cool dip in the swimming pool.

Unforgettable memories are sure to touch your hearts at this timeless inn. Enjoy!

Guestroom rates: $75.00 ~ $130.00
1804 South Park Street • Brenham, Texas 77833
409.836.1672 • 888.FAR.VIEW
E.mail: Farview@phoenix.net   Fax: 409.836.5893

Nueces Canyon Ranch & Lodgings

Discover the way Texas used to be when you visit this 135 acre ranch nestled in the rolling hills and green meadows of rural Washington County. This working cattle ranch with hundreds of cattle and beautiful cutting horses is an adventure to be remembered.

Miles of hiking and riding trails are an inspiration to search out the perfect picnic spot as you stroll along small lakes and flowing streams. In the evening, enjoy the romantic Grand Restaurant with white table cloths and three huge chandeliers. Prime rib, steaks, baked red fish and chicken breasts are part of the menu.

Bed and Breakfast accommodations include three rooms that have scenic views of fields and forests. All are individually decorated, there are country antiques and a delicious touch of the fanciful. Luxurious terry cloth robes are provided, and a generous continental breakfast is included with your stay.

The Inn at Nueces Canyon Ranch has twelve rooms with private baths, TV's, and luxurious furnishings. In the morning, the breakfast bar is yours to enjoy in the Hospitality Room. A beautiful swimming pool is available to all guests.

Guests can go horseback riding if they are experienced in horsemanship. Practice under the shade of the arena, or in the 150 ft. round, outdoor training corral. When you feel comfortable with your horse, discover many nice trails that lead through the scenic countryside. A truly marvelous experience, the gate is always open to all "friends" that visit the tranquil surroundings of this estate.

Guestroom rates: $75.00 ~ $90.00 • Handicapped facilities available
9501 U.S. Highway 290 West • Brenham, Texas 77833
409.289.5300 ~ 800.925.5058 ~ Fax: 409.289.2411
http://www.nuecescanyon.com

Love Note...

Just about every weekend, there are horse shows in the covered stage area at Nueces Canyon. Relax in bleachers and watch registered breed and NCHA cutting competitions that sometimes run all night. Best of all... it's free!

Mariposa Ranch

*H*ere is a delightful journey into the beautiful countryside of Brenham! If you are in search of an escape from the city, Mariposa Ranch is your prescription to peace and solitude. Located on 100 acres, this working ranch is a pleasure to visit.

As you approach this property, you'll delight in the picture perfect setting of a wood fence, an open field, and cattle grazing peacefully away. Pulling into the driveway, you will see four additional historical houses tucked among the trees. Upon your arrival, a cheerful greeting is extended to you by the family cats and dogs. In fact, you can't help but think that you are "Coming Home".

All of the afore-mentioned houses are individual in their own right. Let's explore...

The Main Guest House is an 1870 Plantation home and has two spacious rooms with 12' ceilings, queen size beds and private baths. The Texas Ranger Cabin is an authentic 1825 log cabin complete with huge stone fireplace, clawfoot tub and upstairs loft with queen size bed. Fern Oaks Cottage, a quaint "Honeymoon Cottage", has a queen size bed, fireplace and cozy porch. The Independence House was built in 1836, the year Texas proclaimed its independence from Mexico. It contains two luxurious suites, each with a very a large bedroom and study, two fireplaces are in each suite and private baths have clawfoot tubs.

Should you desire a break from the world, arrangements can be made for a massage, manicure, or pedicure in the privacy of your quarters. Mariposa Ranch also offers a special romantic package called An Enchanting Evening® – a beautiful game for couples to share. Designed for couples who delight in surprising one another, this game has been known to inspire many an unforgettable evening.

After a restful night's sleep in the country, enjoy a delicious country breakfast, wander around the property and then curl up for a nap. You are sure to leave rested, relaxed and rejuvenated!

> **MARIPOSA RANCH**
> Guestroom rates: $75.00 – $140.00
> Route 4, Box 172 • Brenham, Texas 77833
> 409.836.4737 ~ 409.836.4575

108 · Romantic Texas

Houston

I met her in the greenest dells
Where dew drops pearl the wood bluebells
The lost breeze kissed her bright blue eye
The bee kissed and went singing by
A sunbeam found a passage there
A gold chain round her neck so fair
As secret as the wild bee's song
She lay there all the summer long

~ *John Clare – Song (Secret Love)*

Houston

A diversified and sprawling city rich in culture and history, Houston is accented with stunning modern skyscrapers, greenery, flowers and spacious parks. An extensive collection of restaurants and nightclubs offer a variety of entertainment for people of all ages. Cultural activities include art galleries, stage productions, outdoor performances at the Miller Outdoor Theater in Hermann Park, the Museum of Fine Arts, Contemporary Art Museum, and the Menil Art Collection. The Houston Symphony performs at the Wortham Theater Center, the site of Sesque Centennial Park which has an elegant contemporary waterfall. This is the perfect backdrop for a picnic during the day. At night, you may see a romantic couple stealing kisses on the steps adjacent to the waterfall.

Nature lovers will delight in Mercer Arboretum and Botanic Gardens; a 225 acre preserve with trails leading through East Texas Piney woods and 14 acres of landscaped gardens. The Houston Arboretum has inspiring forest trails, and the Armand Bayou Nature Center displays 2100 acres of marsh, forest, bayou and prairie. The teahouse at the Japanese gardens overlook a waterfall cascading over pink Texas granite blocks. The Zoological Gardens feature a unique tropical aviary with more than 200 exotic birds.

A visit to the Cockrell Butterfly Center is a must! This six story glass pyramid surrounds a tropical rainforest with pathways that lead through colourful flowers, medicinal plants, giant trees, a 40 ft. waterfall and of course... thousands of butterflies! Be sure to visit the Transco Tower Wall of Water sculpture in the Galleria Shopping area. This is especially nice at night.

Special occasion? Jordan Limousine features a 1937 Rolls Royce and an assortment of antique cars that are guaranteed to delight your sweetheart. 713.680.3181. Two favourite romantic destinations include the La Tour D'Argent Restaurant, an early 1900s log cabin. Here, fine French Cuisine is served in a multi level huntsman setting with large picture windows looking onto an exquisite garden. A fireplace and a harpist add the finishing romantic touch. Most romantic table: 43. Average price per person $20.00 – $30.00, 2011 Ella Blvd. ~ 713.864.9864. Marfreless is a cozy bar that has comfy sofas, low lights and classical music in the background. The perfect Romantic Rendezvous. 2006 Pedan Ave. 713.528.0083. Convention & Visitors Bureau: 713.227.3100

Angel Arbor Bed & Breakfast Inn

Houston's historic Heights Boulevard is graced by the presence of this Georgian styled Angel Arbor Bed & Breakfast Inn. Located just five minutes from downtown Houston, Angel Arbor offers a perfect blend of convenience, comfort, beauty and tranquility in an atmosphere guaranteed to satisfy the most romantic to the most practical of guests. The inn derives its name from the two primary features of the backyard garden, an artfully placed angel statue and a vine laden arbor. Angel Arbor's first floor boasts an antique filled parlor, a reading room and gracious formal dining room as well as a sunroom for game playing or casual dinning. A wicker furnished solarium overlooks the beautiful, manicured garden.

Upstairs, the three spacious bedrooms, each with a name inspired by an angel, fulfill the promise of a heavenly night's rest. Visitors willing to leave the comfort of their rooms may relax on the spacious balcony secure beneath a blanket of stars and giant pecan trees. The Angelique Room, furnished with a queen cherry sleigh bed and cozy love seat is sure to delight with its private bath complete with a garden view. The Gabriel Room, rich with its luxurious deep burgundy accents, looks down upon the boulevard with its wide esplanade and walking trail. The fleecy cloud of the hand crocheted bed canopy and the invitation to tea for two are the highlighted attractions of the Raphael Room.

Guests of Angel Arbor enjoy a full memorable breakfast served daily by innkeeper Marquerite Swanson and amenities which include cable TV, in-room phones and luxury soaps, lotions and bathrobes.

ANGEL ARBOR BED & BREAKFAST INN
Guestroom rates: $100.00 ~ $119.00
848 Heights Boulevard • Houston, Texas 77007
713.868.4654 ~ 800.722.8788

Romantic Texas · 111

The Highlander

Nestled among stately pecan trees in lovely Woodland Heights is a tranquil neighborhood located on the edge of downtown Houston. Built as a basic four square in 1922 and lovingly maintained by previous owners, The Highlander has been redecorated extensively by the present owners, Georgie and Arlen McIrvin.

An appreciated retreat with three guestrooms, each decorated with romance in mind. The style is unique and creative. All rooms have fresh flowers, lace, ceiling fans, plush robes and a private bath. A television room allows you to enjoy the day at your leisure. Complimentary coffee and soft drinks are available.

The picturesque garden has a large gazebo with skylights and is ideal for bird and squirrel watching any time of the day. Consider an intimate wedding in this secret garden among twinkle lights, candles and the shimmering stars above. Marriage and romance are honored and celebrated at The Highlander, and an experienced wedding coordinator is available.

A full breakfast is served in the dining room with china, crystal and silver, or it may be served in the gazebo. Specialties include poached pears in raspberry sauce, fluffy omelets and heart shaped homemade buttermilk biscuits.

For those who love the Art of Romance, you must experience; An Enchanting Evening® – a beautiful game for couples to share. Created for those who delight in surprising one another, this game inspires intimate moments of love. It goes like this...

Upon your return from a romantic dinner in town, you come back to your room to discover the soft glow of candlelight, a bottle of non-alcoholic champagne and roses. Set up on your bed will be a delightful board game that includes; intimate question answering, new ways of touching, champagne toasts and general relationship exploring. The first player to complete a full circuit around the board can have a wish fulfilled! Speculation is that this game takes about two hours and that depends on you!

Guestroom rates: $80.00 ~ $95.00 ~
Call ahead for more details on An Enchanting Evening®
607 Highland Avenue • Houston, Texas 77009
713.861.6110 ~ 800.807.6110
http://www.gotexas.com/highlander/index.html
EMail: highlander@iapc.net

Vargos

A truly magical restaurant, this Houston landmark is famous for hosting memorable weddings, receptions, bridal showers and rehearsal dinners. An exquisite setting is enhanced by a private lake, acres of magnificent gardens, graceful swans and strolling peacocks. You are sure to enjoy a romantic candlelit dinner seated by picture windows with panoramic views of illuminated footpaths, suspended bridges, towering trees and rolling hills. Begin your diner with Escargot Bourguignon, Stuffed Quail or Oriental Chicken Salad, and then enjoy a main course of Long Island Duck Breast, Snapper Vera Cruz, or a delicious Pork Chop New Orleans. Pasta, steaks seafood and fowl are part of this menu and all are guaranteed to satisfy your tastebuds. After dinner, explore the romantic setting of this property. There are many Kissing Spots and a number of benches inspire intimate moments in time.

Average price per person: $13.00 – $25.00
Excluding tax, gratuity and tip.
2401 Fondren • Houston, Texas 77063 • 713.782.3888

Mesa

A fun excursion any time of the day, this restaurant specializes in delightful treats with a Southwestern flair. Although there is indoor seating, the outdoor patio, accented by a soothing water fountain, is the best place to sit. All of the food served here is exceptional and while deciding what to eat, try the Passion Fruit ice tea or Blue Margaritta. For starters, sample the sweet potato chips with Quemade sauce, (you can't eat just one) or the Crab Cakes with Pepper Cilantro sauce. For a main course, the Angel Hair with Shrimp in goat cheese cream and Mariscos; bacon wrapped jumbo shrimp, are house favourites. The Mixed Grill; beef tenderloin and crab cake is very tasty. By special request, you can have it stuffed with Kotija with Monterey Jack cheese. Yummy! Desserts include the Jack Daniels pie, Honey Flam with Mango and Raspberry sauces, or the Chocolate Mousse taco. Finish your experience with a Mesacuines Coffee – a real treat! And don't forget, the Sunday Brunch is incredible!

Average price per person: $19.00 – $12.00
Excluding tax, gratuity and tip.

Patrician

A large three story mansion built in 1919, this Colonial Revival style home was originally owned by a prominent Houston attorney. The new owner, Pat Thomas has lovingly restored this home to its former grandeur and offers overnight accommodations at affordable rates.

Enter the house to the sounds of relaxing background music coming from an intimate living room with a fireplace. There is a solarium with tile floors that is perfect for meetings or a reception, after a beautiful wedding in the gazebo.

The Inn has three rooms and two suites, all with one-of-a-kind antiques, private bath with a clawfoot tub, and antique four poster beds. The upstairs master bedroom is a very spacious room and features an Eastlake queen size bed and private bath.

Breakfast is served gourmet style in the dining room and may include creamy French Toast, homemade coffee cakes, apple pancakes, fresh squeezed juice and fruit.

If you plan on exploring the sights of Houston, The Patrician is centrally located and within walking distance of the Museum of Fine Arts, Hermann Park and Rice University. Rice University. On occasion, a Murder Mystery Dinner takes place in the house, allowing couples the opportunity to participate in a very unique experience.

1200 Southmore Boulevard • Houston, Texas 77004
713.523.1114 ~ 800.553.5797
Guestroom rates: $79.00 ~ $99.00

BED AND BREAKFAST RESERVATION CENTER

Pat Thomas also has a Bed and Breakfast Reservation Service that deals with many properties throughout Texas. They include traditional B&Bs, a mix of the old and the new. Some are in the country, even on working ranches and many are situated on the water, lakes and rivers. 713.523.1114

Lancaster Hotel

What a delightful surprise in the heart of downtown Houston! The Lancaster Hotel is a 1926 thirteen story historic property that underwent a complete renovation in 1982. As you approach the beautiful entranceway with burgundy awnings and brass and beveled glass, you are graciously greeted by the hotel doorman. Upon entering, an intimate British-style lobby displays a fine European elegance not found in larger hotels. Recognized as Houston's only small luxury hotel, the personal ambiance of this hotel will appeal to those who appreciate the finer things in life.

Each of the eighty-four guest rooms and nine suites are draped in rich tones of crimson, hunter green and rose and are decorated in imported English fabrics and wallpapers. Luxurious poster beds, executive desks and mahogany armoires with mini-bars, cable television and video players are finishing touches. A library of videocassettes, complementary limousine service and The Texas Club, an on-property state of the art health facility, are available to all guests. A personal favourite, The Lancaster Hotel is truly a romantic destination point.

LANCASTER HOTEL
Guestroom rates: 185.00 ~ 550
Corporate and weekend rates available.

Bistro Lancaster

This on-property restaurant serves outstanding food for breakfast, lunch, dinner, pre-theatre and late-night dining. Chef Louis Cressy creates his own interpretation of Gulf Coast cooking that combines southern fare, rich Creole spices and a wide cultural mix of foods from Texas to the Yucatan. An antique bar in the restaurant is a relaxing spot to have a drink.

BISTRO LANCASTER
Average price per person: Lunch $9.00 – $17.00,
Dinner: $15.95 – $24.95
701 Texas Avenue at Louisiana • Houston, Texas, 77002-2794
713.228.9500 ~ 800.231.0336 ~ Fax: 713.223.4528

Durham House
Bed & Breakfast Inn

Even from first glance at the cupid weathervane perched high atop the turret of this Queen Anne Victorian, the suggestion of romance is readily apparent. A front porch swing beckons to loving couples and the backyard gazebo offers the perfect spot for a moonlit conversation or an intimate wedding ceremony.

Upstairs in the main house the Rose Room with its 1860 walnut Victorian bed and its enchanting bathroom featuring a glorious bevelled glass window, a favourite with almost all guests. An antique wedding dress adorns the wall of the Blue Room with its boulevard view. The unusual shape of the Turret Room makes it seem the perfect place to curl up with a good book and let the world go by.

Downstairs is the parlor and formal dining area and a white wicker filled solarium overlooks the backyard garden and patio.

Tucked neatly beneath the branches of the giant oak and pecan trees at the rear of the property is the Carriage House with three additional guest bedrooms. The Garden Room downstairs boasts a floral and hunter green decor, while the other downstairs room has a Victorian country look with its antique, highback oak bed and nostalgic accessory pieces. The romantic Heart Suite which occupies the entire second floor is the delight of all couples who visit. One entire wall is covered with heart motif collectibles, everything from old postcards and Valentines to dainty heart shaped cushions and hat pins. The small round table and two chairs provide the opportunity for in-room dining for couples desiring the finishing touch of privacy in this delightful hide-away.

Guestroom rates: $65.00 ~ $95.00
921 Heights Blvd. • Houston, Texas, 77008
713.868.4654 ~ 800.722.8788

Out & About
The Gulf Coast

Beautiful days and friends
To share the fun of summer sun.
Beautiful days and friends
Make castles in the sand
Walk the beach, hand-in-hand.
Beautiful days and friends
Never come to an end   You are my friend
~ Jamie Ehret

Captain's Quarters

Nestled on a bluff of Galveston Bay, Captains Quarters is a journey into a luxurious and elegant past. Reminiscent of an early American whaler's home on the rugged New England coast, as you pass through the welcoming doors of this estate you will discover a warmly decorated interior full of beautiful antiques.
Owner Mary Patterson invites you to enjoy the beauty of this establishment which features ten foot beamed ceilings, stained glass windows and collectors art. A semi-holiday theme is incorporated throughout the house and it is especially nice at... Christmas!
The magnificent dining room and spacious living room feature large picture windows that overlook the ocean. The adjacent outdoor veranda is an ideal place to watch a full moon rise on the water. In the winter, relax in the living room by the fireplace and savour the gracious warmth of true southern hospitality.
You can choose from five guest rooms that are all furnished with antiques. Each has its own luxurious bath, the two rooms upstairs have views of the ocean. A restful night of sleep is guaranteed as you drift away to the soothing sounds of the surf breaking on the shore. In the morning, a gourmet breakfast is served on delicate china in the formal dining room in front of a crackling fire.
Lazy days are encouraged here and there are a number of things to do. Enjoy a picnic on the lawn adjacent to the water, lounge on the spacious veranda as you watch the sailboats pass by, or explore the quaint downtown area of Kemah. Feeling adventurous? Discover the intimate spiral stairway leading to the Widows Walk on the fifth floor, the highest point in Kemah.
The perfect setting for special events, honeymoons and anniversaries, your comfort is the utmost priority at Captains Quarters. Guaranteed!

CAPTAIN'S QUARTERS
Guestroom rates: $55.00 ~ $120.00
701 Bay Avenue • Kemah, Texas
77565 • 713.334.4141

Kemah

The gateway to the bay, Kemah is a small paradise nestled in a half-moon pocket on Galveston Bay. It was founded in 1889 by John Henry Jipp, a veteran of the Magnolia Rangers. Home to a premiere marina complex, day-sailing and fishing expeditions, exploring this area is just part of the fun. Unique craft and antique shops intertwine with fine art galleries to inspire an afternoon of exploration. The rush of everyday living disappears as visitors stroll through this quaint town while seeking out unusual finds. Restaurants abound and you are sure to find some of the finest seafood in Texas served in this area. In fact, searching out the perfect dining establishment to suit your mood can be a fun adventure. Here are a few favourites; Landry's Seafood House is a very popular spot and the second floor veranda is very elegant and romantic ~ 713.334.2413, Joe Lee's is a casual setting and has a nice outdoor patio that overlooks the water ~ 713.334.3711, The Flying Dutchman has two outdoor patios, upstairs and downstairs. Both with excellent views ~ 713.334.7575, and Joe's Crab Shack is unquestionably a party atmosphere and also has a large outdoor patio. A variety of one-of-a-kind knickknacks are throughout and many hang from the ceiling ~ 713.334.2881. Caludio's is very romantic and has a piano bar.

Galveston Island

An historic city that began as a thriving port in the mid 1800s, Galveston offers a variety of things to do for new explorers. The Great Storm of 1900 laid waste to the city as a relentless hurricane drove an angry ocean before it, covering the island from Gulf to Bay. Although it was said that Galveston was "history", reconstruction began immediately after and it is still recognized as a major port to this very day.

Citywide celebrations include Christmas on the Strand and Mardi Gras, a rousing celebration that livens up the city in February. The Outdoor Amphitheater in Galveston Island State Park is another great destination where you can watch live musicals under the stars. This is a magical summer experience that you are sure to remember! Afterwards, take a walk in the park until the traffic dies down. ~ 800.54.SHOWS. A tour of the Moody Mansion will bring a sparkle to the eyes of those who appreciate the opulence of the Victorian era. 2618 Broadway ~ 409.762.7668.

The Historic Strand District ~ Featuring some of the nation's finest collection of restored Victorian architecture, this area is filled with a versatile selection of unique antique shops, art galleries and restaurants. A full day of discovery is guaranteed for those who enjoy shopping or browsing. Old Galveston Square has a lot of neat shops and a beautiful stairway leads you to the second floor. Admire the intricate balcony railings and then steal a kiss in the antique elevator. The Strand Soda Fountain is another trip into the past where you can watch hand-made fudge being made and an 80 year old Taffy Puller machine that still works! This is a great place to spend time searching out an assortment of bins filled with all kinds of goodies.

The Mardi Gras Museum consists of three galleries with an impressive display of local Mardi Gras memorabilia. 2211 Strand ~ 409.763.1133. Don't forget to visit the 1894 Grand Opera House which has live entertainment throughout the year. Indulge yourselves in a self-guided tour of the exquisite theater and delight in the double curved balconies and the intricate craftsman throughout. Many famous entertainers have performed here over the years including George Burns and Gracie Allen, John Philip Sousa and the Marx Brothers. 220 Postoffice Street ~ 800.821.1894

Star Drug Store is the oldest Drug store in Texas and has an old fashioned Ice Cream Parlor, dining counter, a fabulous display of antique medicines and the oldest neon Coca-cola sign in existence. The Limeade is great! 510 23rd Street ~ 409.762.8658. Mama Nifas Mexican Restaurant has a sun room and an outdoor patio. Both are perfect for a lazy afternoon lunch or casual dinner. On the weekends, Mariachi bands liven up the setting. 2215 Strand ~ 409.770.0029

Pier 21 ~ A shipwatchers paradise in Galveston's port, this destination point includes museums, shops and restaurants. A multi-image documentary of The Great Storm can be seen here and next door at Pier 22, pick your catch of the day at Fisherman's Wharf. Or enjoy fresh seafood dining indoors or outdoors at one of many restaurants. Afterwards, take a tour of Galveston's historic waterfront aboard the tour boat Seagull that departs from this pier. Upon your return, sample specialty beers at The Strand Brewery.

Love Note...

The Rainforest Pyramid in Moody Gardens is a ten-story glass pyramid with a self-contained environment that brings you into the jungles and the rainforest of Asia, Africa and the Americas. A full acre of natural wonders include waterfalls, cliffs, caverns and a stunning Mayan Colonnade (this is another great Kissing Spot). ~ 800.582.4673

Madame Dryer's Bed And Breakfast

A unique way to enjoy a traditional Victorian Bed and Breakfast in Galveston, this is an experience with many special touches. Here you can enjoy the feeling of elegance from the past and still appreciate the luxury, comfort and pleasures of today. Located in the East End Historic District, this B&B is surrounded by beautiful Victorian homes in a quaint neighborhood.

As you enter this faithfully restored home built in 1889, you will notice the period details such as wrap-around porches, high airy ceilings, hard wood floors and lace curtains. Each room is furnished with delightful antiques that bring back memories of days gone by. Ashten's Room is a large room at the top of the beautiful oak stairway and is furnished with a queen-size bed of carved oak. Two comfortable chairs and other antiques combine to make this a truly elegant room for that special occasion. The adjoining private bath has a walk-in shower, a spacious vanity with double sinks and access to the top porch. Blakes Room has a queen-size bed set in a bay window, with a delicately crocheted bedspread, wonderful English antique furnishings and a private bath down the hall with a deep claw-foot tub ideal to relax in. Corbin's Room has an adjoining bathroom with a claw-foot tub and features a king-size poster bed and a tile fireplace with an oak mantel with a mirror. Antique dolls, whimsical old hats and floral swags adorn this delightful room.

A gourmet breakfast is served in the elegant dining room on formal place settings. Relaxing moments can be spent on the front porch, or enjoy a pleasant ride to the beach or the Strand Historic District on bicycles that are supplied. By prior arrangement, a horse drawn carriage will pick you up at the front door, tour the historic district and then bring you to one of many fine restaurants nearby. A very memorable experience, Madame Dryer's is one of this authors favourite establishments.

MADAME DRYER'S BED AND BREAKFAST
Guestroom rates: $90.00 ~ $125.00
1720 Postoffice Street • Galveston, Texas 77550
409.765.5692

Tremont House

*L*ocated in the heart of Galveston's historic Strand District, the Tremont House allows you the opportunity to take a step back in time to the grandness of the Victorian era. Built in 1879, the neo-Renaissance design of this building inspires closer inspection during your stay. Modern conveniences are at your fingertips and an efficient staff ensures that your stay is an adventure into the Art of Romance.

Upon entering the four-story atrium lobby, admire the massive skylight that bathes the inside of the hotel with an inviting glow. The imposing Toujouse Bar has an ornate mahogany bar and in the evening, a Champagne Hour is enlivened by old-time favourites on the piano.

117 guest rooms have polished hardwood floors, custom woven rugs, antique replica four-poster wooden beds or brass beds, Victorian armoires and hand painted Italian tiles in the bathrooms. Some rooms are graced by charming wood columns original to the building. Rooms on the perimeter of the atrium have double French doors that lead out to ironwork balconies that overlook the lobby. Rooms on the outer perimeter of the building have views of the Strand Historic District. As you can imagine, a stay at this hotel is an experience you will not soon forget. The magical setting of the Tremont Hotel is bound to inspire romance.

Guestroom rates: $135.00 – $375.00 Packages available
2300 Ship's Mechanic Row • Galveston, Texas 77550-1520

☆ Lone Star Rendezvous ✦✦✦

Looking for something to do? A variety of restaurants are yours to enjoy. The Merchant Prince is a cozy little niche with a trickling fountain; The Wentletrap serves Continental cuisine in an elegant setting; Trumpets on the Strand offers Southwestern cuisine and live entertainment in a casual atmosphere; and Fitzpatrick is Galveston's only Irish pub and serves a light bill of fare. Fresh-baked delights are yours to enjoy at the Phoenix Bakery and Coffee House, Sa'saparila Ice Cream Parlor invites you to remember your youth, and from the Rooftop Terrace, you can watch the sunset while ships from around the world dock in Galveston's port.

Hotel Galvez

Another trip into the past, the Hotel Galvez, constructed in 1911, is the end result of the indomitable spirit of Galvestonians who survived the devastating Great Storm of 1900. Restored in 1995, the original ambiance of the turn-of-the-century still prevails. Viewed from afar, Hotel Galvez is reminiscent of a grand European castle. The main entrance is lined with towering palm trees, and upon further exploration, you will delight in the lushly landscaped grounds. A trellis-covered arcade wall, accented by shell basins, is the finishing touch to the pool area that has a swim-up bar and heated spa.

225 guestrooms and three suites offer panoramic views of the area. All are decorated with soothing pastel colours that complement your views of the ocean. A two-level Penthouse Suite features a game room, a spacious bedroom, living room and dining room.

During your stay, relax on the glass-enclosed terrace of The Veranda or enjoy light snacks while basking in the summer sun at the Seaside Grill. Bernardo's feature's traditional and nouvelle cuisine and has beautiful views of the beach. Club Galvez is a popular venue for live entertainment and you can dance to the sounds of local bands every Friday and Saturday evening. Both are located on the property.

Many special packages are available and include; Bed & Breakfast, Bed & Brunch, Sentimental Journey, Unforgettable Honeymoon and of course...The Perfect Honeymoon! A world like no other along the Texas coast, Hotel Galvez is truly a glorious island escape.

Guestroom rates: $110.00 – $350.00 Packages available
2024 Seawall Boulevard • Galveston, Texas 77550

Love Note...

The glass pyramid in Moody Gardens is a ten-story glass pyramid with a self-contained environment that takes you into the jungles and the rainforest of Asia, Africa and the Americas. A full acre of natural wonders include waterfalls, cliffs, caverns and a stunning Mayan Colonnade. Another great Kissing Spot. ~ 800.582.4673

Brazoria

A truly romantic experience awaits you when you visit this area. Forget shopping or exploring, an unforgettable experience is yours by doing two simple things; savour a wonderful Bed & Breakfast experience at Roses And The River and then have dinner at Dido's. Both are in country settings with views of towering trees and the San Bernard River (a popular destination point for water enthusiasts on the weekends, this river becomes a peaceful paradise during the week).

As you are driving to Dido's you will realize that getting there is half the fun! You'll enjoy this excursion through mature forests delicately lined with wildflowers along the roadside. Upon your arrival, you will discover a casual restaurant with a wonderful outdoor patio. Here you can take in the panoramic scenery while enjoying fresh seafood or steaks. A docked paddleboat is the finishing touch to this picturesque setting. Afterwards, enjoy a walk on the property, or sit on the dock and watch the stars above. This is a great Kissing Spot!

$9.00 – $12.00 per person. ~ 409.964.3167

Palacios

Nestled on the Texas coast midway between Galveston and Corpus Christi on Tres Palacios Bay, this part of the state boasts many marinas, parks, and an airport with a 5,000 foot runaway. Fishing, birding, golfing and sailing are all popular activities, while seven miles of shoreline is an inspiration to a walk on the beach. Be sure to discover the seawall walking path. How about a picnic in the waterfront park while watching the shrimping fleet go by? At night, lighted fishing piers paint a reflected picture of romance.

Located along the Central Flyway, there are five birding sites in the city and six more nearby. The Pavilion is a round open-air structure that sits elegantly in Palacios' South Bay. This is a fine Romantic Rendezvous as the moon rises on the horizon. There is a Fourth of July Waterfront Carnival, and September Bay Fest is always a popular excursion. All in all, Palacios offers a variety of activities for those searching for a break from the city.

Roses And The River

*A*nother great escape to the country, this B&B is only an hour's drive from Houston and Galveston. Nestled along the banks of the San Bernard River and surrounded by the fragrance of a beautiful rose garden, Roses and the River is a private world you are sure to enjoy.

Long outdoor verandas, furnished with comfortable rockers and overhead fans overlook the river. At night under starry skies, this isolated property is an absolutely magical spot. The night of a full moon allows the opportunity for a romantic stroll on a country road ~ the perfect place to steal a kiss.

Upstairs are three guest rooms and each has a queen size bed, private bath, television and VCR. Named for a favourite rose, they all have their own distinct personality. New Dawn welcomes the first light of day on the river, Rise 'n Shine is a cheery yellow room that overlooks the water. Rainbow's End is a bright, colourful room and reflects the rainbow hues seen in the rose garden. This room has bedroom and bathroom window seats that provide private nooks perfect for reading, or day dreaming. The beautiful bathroom has a one-of-a-kind, custom-made, claw-foot spa tub which is a true pleasure to experience.

During the day, rest in the shade of tall oak trees on spacious lawns, or on the deck overlooking the river. On cool winter nights relax in front of the fireplace in the living room. Here, rest and relaxation allow for peaceful moments.

The San Bernard River is a popular retreat for water enthusiasts on the weekend; if you have your own boat or water sports equipment, docking facilities are available at the B&B from a nearby public boat launch.

A delicious country breakfast is served in the beautiful dining area where you can enjoy specialties like blushing orange cooler, grapefruit baked Alaska and cheese blintz souffle with fruit sauce. With a picturesque view of the river, this is the perfect to way to begin your day. The breeze is blowing, the sun is shining and everything is just magical!

Guestroom rates: $125.00
7074 CR 506 • Brazoria, Texas 77522 • 409.798.1070
800.610.1070 ~ Fax: 409.798.1070 • Internet: hosack@tgn.net

Moonlight Bay

In 1910, Mrs. Opal Price gave beautiful parties in her elegant home on the waterfront in Palacios. Music from the bandstand of the nearby Pavilion wafted over the eaves, entertaining guests in long white skirts and straw hats on the porches of Mrs. Price's fine home.

Now known as Moonlight Bay, this wonderful house has come alive again under the careful hand of Miss Gaye Rogers. Accomplished pianist, gourmet cook and talented interior designer, Miss Rogers has named her B&B after one of her favourite songs, Moonlight Bay.

This house has been beautifully restored and guests are sure to appreciate its fine hospitality. Moonlight and Roses, which overlooks the bay from two balconies has antique furnishings and is a favourite for honeymooners. Moonglow has trellis design wallpaper, a beautiful bower with twin loveseats, and a "surprise" door that opens onto an enclosed balcony. Ebbtide features a garden atmosphere and you can see the treetops in the windows from its en suite bath.

The Paper Moon Vacation Guest House has three rooms with full guest baths en suite; A Gift From the Sea is a dreamy room that may inspire writing a novel, The Sand Piper has spectacular views of the bay and The Great Gatsby has a fireplace and a romantic four poster column king sized bed. Original murals on every wall reflect a by-gone era of fun and frolic. French author, Colette would be pleased to see her story lines so cleverly portrayed.

The spacious living room is always a favourite gathering spot and offers spectacular bay views. A fireplace adds a cozy warmth on winter evenings. In the morning, guests enjoy a gourmet breakfast served formally in the oriental dining room. After breakfast, enjoy a morning stroll on the seawall and then relax with a good book in the library. Afternoon tea is served at 4:00pm. During this time, Miss Rogers performs live piano music from the 1940s.

A relaxing retreat by the bay with a delightful atmosphere of casual elegance and a fine harmony of wonderful food, music and hospitality, you are sure to have a memorable stay at this B&B.

Guestroom rates: $65.00 – $100.00
506 South Bay Boulevard • Palacios, Texas 77465
512.972.2232 ~ 800.714.1997 x51 ~ E-Mail: grogers@sat.net

Corpus Christi

Although there are a number of skyscrapers and a thriving downtown business center here, upon further exploration, you realize that this is just another small town. Interesting excursions include the Marina, The Texas State Aquarium and the U.S.S, Lexington museum; a massive aircraft carrier that has daily tours. Afterwards, enjoy a walk on the picturesque beach just south of the museum. Take a trip back in time and tour Heritage Park where there are nine restored historic homes dating from 1852 – 1910. Guided tours: 512.883.0639.

• Ramada Hotel Bayfront ~ This is a very affordable hotel in downtown Corpus Christi. 200 guest rooms are nicely furnished and have a private balcony, many with bayfront views. A swimming pool is available, and the Atrium Lounge is a garden-like atmosphere that features daily drink specials, hors d'oeuvres and live entertainment. Palm's restaurant is in a casual setting where you can enjoy breakfast, lunch or a relaxing dinner. A Romantic Rendezvous special includes a Bayview room, a bottle of champagne and fruit tray upon your arrival. You also receive a gift certificate for $20.00 towards dinner in the hotel restaurant (or room service), a full breakfast for two, a free movie of your choice and of course... a Do Not Disturb sign! Price: Only $99.00

601 North Water Street • Corpus Christi, Texas, 78402
512.882.8100 ~ 800.688.0334

Port Royal ~A beachfront resort on Mustang Island, this property has over twenty-five acres of unique grounds in a lush tropical setting. The rooms are spacious and comfortable and have balconies that look onto the Gulf or pool area. All have kitchens, living areas with built in stereo system, cable TV and wetbar. Master suites have whirlpool tubs. The expansive Royal Blue Lagoon Pool has hidden grottos, waterslide, four whirlpool spas, three tropical waterfalls and two swim-up cabana bars. A private boardwalk leads over the dunes and onto the beach – a great excursion at night. Ask about the romance package! Rates vary by season

6317 Sate Highway 361 • Port Aransas, Texas 78373
800.242.1034

Fortuna Bay Bed & Breakfast

What a refreshing surprise minutes away from ocean! Nestled at the intersection of five canals leading to the Laguna Madre and the Gulf of Mexico, you have bayside views of the beautiful white sands of North Padre Island from this property. Owners John and Jackie Fisher encourage you to enjoy the restful surroundings of their grounds.

Driving to this delightful hideaway through the winding streets of a quiet bayside neighborhood is half of the fun. Upon discovering this three story condominium with a red tiled roof, you know you have found a harmonious escape from the outside world. Here you can swim in the pool, fish off the deck, or play golf at Padre Island Country Club.

Two suites are available for guests and include all the amenities (and more) of a Bed and Breakfast Inn. In fact, it is almost like belonging to a small, quiet country club. Each suite has a plentiful supply of fresh flowers, a large bedroom with queen-size bed, living room with television, and kitchen with microwave.

If you are feeling adventurous, John is happy to take you on a boating excursion through the canals in the late afternoon or early evening. You are sure to delight in the many beautiful homes and picturesque views on this unforgettable journey.

A feel of the Caribbean Islands is emphasized by the soothing sounds of the many local, and migrating birds. Spectacular sunset views from the deck inspire a romantic moment and in the morning enjoy an extended continental breakfast on the patio tables. The perfect way to begin your day! Truly a home away from home, it just can't get much better than this!

FORTUNA BAY BED & BREAKFAST
Guestroom rates: $96.00
Fortuna Bay Co. ~ Route 4, Box 115P1
Robstown, Texas, 78380
512.387.5666

Favourite local dining establishments in Port Aransas include, Beulah's, Tortuga Flats and Trout Street Station, a new establishment with a very quaint atmosphere. Snoopy's, serves fresh seafood and has an old fashioned ice cream parlor. This is an ideal meeting spot any time of the year.

Padre Island National Seashore ~ Located along the south coast of Texas, east of Corpus Christi, this sparkling preserve embraces 70 miles of white sand beaches, picturesque windswept dunes, and wild landscapes of grasslands and tidal flats. Swimming and sunbathing can be enjoyed almost all year. Many of these beaches are deserted after nightfall and an isolated sand dune may be an inspiration to romance (be sure to bring a blanket). With the stars sparkling brightly above, an unforgettable moment in time is guaranteed! P.S. Full moon rises on the ocean are always spectacular. Check the newspapers for moonrise times and dates.

Port Aransas, Mustang Island & Padre Island ~ Here is a fun excursion...Take 181 to Aransas Pass a ferry takes your car to Port Aransas. An 8 1/2 mile paved road leads to Mustang Island and a beach that you can drive on. After Milepost 5, you can continue through Padre Island for another 55 miles in a four wheel drive vehicle. Consider a camping trip where you will see clear night skies and unforgettable sunrises (or moonrises). Wake in the morning to the sights and sounds of waves crashing on the shore. Park rangers 512.937.2621

South Padre Island

About 2 1/2 hours from Corpus Christi, South Padre Island is a unique experience and a neat little beach town. Although the main focus is the clothing and souvenir shops along the main drag, if you price shop, you can find good deals on beachwear. Beautiful beaches serve as an inspiration to a romantic stroll at night. If you are in an adventurous mood, here are two fun options: Horseback Riding on the Beach is an adventure onto the beaches of the area. Horses are available for all level of riders and a sunset ride on the beach is a must! 800.761.4677. Water Sports Center allows you to enjoy the warm ocean waters on a Jet Ski. Skim the waves with your sweetheart and enjoy the mist of the waters brushing agonist your skin. 210.761.1060
Ferrentino Therapeutic Massage & Reflexology – This is a great gift for your sweetheart, yourself, or for the both of you! A professional massage and/or Aroma Therapy session is conducted by Dolores Ferrentino or, her assistant who help you feel at ease by discussing your massage preferences beforehand. Aching muscles are gently manipulated until you feel like a million dollars. The studio is very nice and relaxing music is conducive to this soothing experience. Couple massages are a specialty or, if this is a special occasion, consider a massage session in the privacy of your hotel room. 1/2 hr: $35.00 ~ 1 hr. $55.00. By appointment. P.O. Box 2403 • South Padre Island, Texas 78597 • 210.761.1814

Bahia Mar Resort

This sub-tropical island resort features a newly renovated 12-story hotel with a host of standard rooms, kitchenettes, or suites, Each room has a private balcony overlooking either the Gulf or the Laguna Madre Bay. Fully equipped two and three bedroom condominiums are also available. Situated on 15 acres of lush beach front property that include two pools, a children's pool, Texas size hot tub, outdoor pool bar and grill, two lighted tennis courts, putting green and beach volleyball courts. This hotel is a great destination point for those in search of a romantic escape. Easy access to the beach makes this a Lone Star favourite, especially at night. Here clear skies and bright, shining stars are an inspiration to unforgettable moments on the sand. Enjoy!

> Guestroom rates: $75.00 – $135.00
> 6300 Padre Boulevard • South Padre Island
> 800.292.7502

Scampi's

Certainly one of the most romantic restaurants in South Padre Island, Scampi's sits on the west side of the peninsula overlooking the water. Beautiful sunset views can be enjoyed from the first floor dining room or the outdoor patio. Delicacies of the house include fresh seafood dishes and the award wining Peanut Butter Shrimp, USDA prime strip steaks, veal, lamb, game and fowl. The Oyster's Rockefeller/Scampis is a must for an appetizer! An extensive wine list features over 200 wines from around the world. After dinner, enjoy the cozy piano bar on the second floor. This is a great place to share intimate moments (and a dance) with your sweetheart! Reservations recommended. Average price per person $12.00 – $17.00
206 West Aries • South Padre Island, Texas 78597 • 210.761.1755

> While on the subject of great stays on the beach, Southern California truly has it's moments. In order to justify a shameless plug for *Romantic Southern California ~ second edition*, here are two favourite excursions in Newport Beach and Catalina Island...

Catalina Island Seacrest Inn

One of Catalina's historic treasures, the Seacrest Inn is overflowing with romance and history. If your desire the romance of a Victorian Style Inn where your amenities can include an in-room whirlpool or tub for two, (complete with rubber duck and bubblebath) then you need search no further. This Inn fulfills those requirements and more.

Originally built as a honeymoon cottage for the Bannings, who owned the island at the turn-of-the-century, this non-smoking B&B retains its tradition as a special place for honeymoons and couples in love. Although fully renovated to modern standards, the leisurely pleasures of the past have been carefully maintained.

With bowers of flowers and lace curtains adorning the Inn from the office to your room, the decor is definitely slanted in favour of those who are romantically inclined. A small mountain of shamed pillows adorn your canopy bed where you will find a Teddy Bear seated comfortably in the center. The spa rooms even have an electric fireplace for that special touch.

Each room is individually climate controlled and include ceiling fans, cable TV (with free movie channels), VCR with Normas' "Mother Approved" video library, refrigerator and a continental breakfast served in the sun room. Don't forget to enjoy the expansive view from the well appointed rooftop sundeck.

♥ An in-house wedding consultant will help you arrange an island wedding or, renewal of your vows (with as little as twenty-four hours notice). Non-denominational wedding services are also available.

Guestroom rates: $95.00 - $185.00
P.O. Box 128 • Avalon, California 90704
310.510.0800 ~ FAX: 310.510.1122
Internet: http://www.catalina.com/seacrest.html
E-Mail: catisle@catalinas.net

BOAT
AND BREAKFAST
Balboa Peninsula

HOW'S THIS FOR AN UNFORGETTABLE romantic experience... a secluded night on a private yacht anchored in beautiful Newport Beach Bay! If you have ever had the fantasy of owning your own yacht and savouring a day, night or weekend in the lap of luxury, the choice is now yours! Or, consider a leisurely cruise to Catalina Island attended by your own professional crew.

A selection of ten yachts and sailboats of varying sizes ranging from 35 to 85 feet in length are part of these one-of-a-kind lodgings. Differing in amenities and decor, all are equipped with showers, TV/VCR, towels and linens. A continental breakfast is included in the price and yours to enjoy in the morning.

Favourite Yachts include: Bounty; one of the most romantic yachts in the fleet, this 1934 sailing vessel is truly a step back into time. A plush interior is complemented by fine teak woods and a dusty rose velvet -- the perfect setting for a "Romantic Rendezvous" with the one you love~ Sheri-Ann; situated in a private corner in Lido Village, cozy evenings and breath-taking views of Newport Harbor are complemented by a fly bridge perfect for sunbathing in complete privacy ~ Victoria offers three elegantly appointed staterooms, decorated in classic antique decor with fine teak and mahogany walls and marble bathroom floors. Searching for an unusual place for a customized party, wedding, anniversary or special occasion? The spacious Bow Wave, Quiet Time or Cassandra yachts may be what you are searching for!

Discover the unparalleled pleasure of spending an evening or entire vacation surrounded by spectacular views, inspirational dawns and romantic sunsets. All this at prices comparable to many hotels or inns. Whatever your desires are, the staff will assist you with reservations and special arrangements to make your stay a memorable one.

BOAT AND BREAKFAST
Yacht rates: $150.00 - $600.00
Cruises range from $60.00 - $400.00 per hour
3400 Via Oporto #103 ♥ Newport Beach, CA ♥ 714.723.5552

Recipes For Romance

I saw your shooting star
As it said good-bye last night
A gypsy on the sands of time
Stardust lost in endless flight

When shadows touch my dreams at night
I'll think of you and smile
A flower in a brave new world
The memory of a shining light

~ Christensen

ROMANTIC DINNERS AT HOME

A book like this would be far from complete without information on this subject. A romantic dinner at home with that special someone is an experience not soon forgotten if done right. The advantage of course is that you are in the privacy of your own home without any distractions. These are tried and true techniques that, if followed closely, will provide an unforgettable evening.

If you have a fireplace, take advantage of it! Nothing sets a mood better than a fire burning in the background. After dinner, mosey over to the sofa, or place large, comfy cushions by the hearth. If you were never a boy scout and have trouble keeping the fire lit, buy one of those fake logs, get it going, and pile real wood around it. No problem!

Romantic music in the background helps to set the mood also. A low key, minimal commercial, radio station works well, but some of the romantic music mentioned earlier in this book, recorded onto long playing tapes, works the best.

Matching table settings are a nice touch. Many elegant utensils and flatware can be purchased at large department stores individually priced. If you keep an eye out for sales, sometimes you can make a score on single place settings, silverware and stemware. Candles, a tablecloth or placemats are a must in order to set the proper atmosphere. For some reason, a romantic dinner without dim lights isn't easy to pull off.

Try to avoid complicated recipes you've never cooked before unless you feel sure you can pull it off. There are many cookbooks in bookstores that offer simple and easy recipes. Some grocery stores also offer a variety of prepared main courses that only need to be placed in an oven. Highlighted with vegetables and fresh bread, you still can have an impressionable meal. Should worse come to worse, and your meal doesn't go as planned, just go with the flow. If the music's good, the lights low, the champagne cold and the company good, the mood will already be set for a marvelous and intimate romantic interlude.

Packing a Picnic Basket

The essentials: A nice picnic basket. Large and small plates -- two each, forks and knives with at least one sharp knife (real cutlery instead of plastic is a nice touch), cloth napkins, wine or champagne glasses and two flat plates to set them on (semi-elegant utensils are preferable and always a nice touch). Don't forget gum or mints.

Now for the fun part...

Find a grocery store with a well-stocked deli and peruse the selections. Be daring and experiment if you're so inclined. A quarter pound each of five or six cheeses and meats will tantalize the taste buds while seafood, pasta or fruit salads, fresh shrimp or oysters add variety. Apples, pears, bananas, strawberries or any other non-messy fruit give a touch of colour to your spread. Request a small container of ice to keep perishables fresh and be sure to remember crackers, French bread and condiments like Grey Poupon to accent your deli selections. ...And lest I forget, Champagne, Wine or Sparkling Cider for that "*romantic*" toast.

That's it! Simple and easy, and bound to please that special someone. If time allows, search out your picnic spots beforehand for the best views and privacy. *Bon Appetít!*

The Impeccable Picnic: A nice blanket to sit on is essential. If you're going to extend the picnic into the evening hours, bring two blankets so that when the evening turns chilly you can sit on top of one and cuddle up under the other. A small vase with flowers is a nice touch. A candle can also add a balanced and polished look, however, if you do use a candle, be sure it's enclosed in some sort of glass container so the wind doesn't blow it out. Don't forget the matches!

Keep in mind that if you do picnic, it's important to know which parks allow glass containers and/or alcohol. Although you probably won't be bothered if you're discreet and in an out of the way area, it's always a good idea to have an enclosed container to hold your bottle. If you really have to, pour your drinks into a plastic bottle beforehand.

Follow the above recommendations and you'll be sure to have an impressive spread that just might win the heart of your date. If what you've put together isn't enough to impress, you may be with the wrong person!

ROMANTIC MOVIES

Casablanca, The African Queen & To Have And Have Not - A personal favourite - Lauren Bacall makes her debut with Bogie. Wow!
Somewhere In Time - Very, romantic!
Age of Innocence - If she had just turned around, his life would have forever changed!
Body Heat - A real steamer with a very interesting twist.
9 1/2 Weeks - If you can ignore the dominant sexist overtones, there are truly some sexy scenes that just might spark an interesting evening.
French Kiss - Great soundtrack also.

On The Lighter Side:
In The Mood - a very funny movie!
The Party with Peter Sellers - what a scream!
Singles - Personal relationships in modern times. An ideal first-time video to watch together.
Honeymoon In Las Vegas - Still an all time favourite.
Grumpy Old Men - The combination of Walter Matthau, Jack Lemmon and Ann-Margret make for a delightful story with a happy ending.
I.Q. - Once again, Walter Matthau (as Albert Einstein) adds a surprisingly nice touch to a very sweet and romantic movie.

And lest we forget...
Sense & Sensibility, Much Ado About Nothing, Only You, Milk Money, While You Were Sleeping, A Walk In The Clouds, Braveheart, The Princess Bride, Love Affair, The Man From Snowy River & The Return To Snowy River, The Philadelphia Story & Brigadoon

ROMANTIC MUSIC

MALE VOCAL - Frank Sinatra's Greatest Hits · Julio Iglesias - "Julio" & "Crazy" · Andy Williams Greatest Hits · Johnny Mathis - Any of his first five albums · Anything by Nat King Cole, Harry Connick Jr. & Luther Vandross.

FEMALE VOCAL - Diana Ross - To Love Again · Sade - Diamond Life · Enya - Watermark · Plus, music by Billie Holiday, Ella Fitzgerald, Anita Baker and Natalie Cole.

SOUNDTRACKS - French Kiss · Much Ado About Nothing, Last of the Mohicans, Dances With Wolves, Edward Scissorhands · Sleepless in Seattle - I could live without "Back in the Saddle Again", but somebody must have thought it was a good idea to include it on the CD.

INSTRUMENTAL
Mystic Moods Orchestra - One Stormy Night - Five stars for this all time classic of beautiful music with a rain storm in the background. · Patrick O'Hearn - Rivers Gonna Rise - New age music perfect for massage sessions. · Enigma - Both CD's are very sensuous and hypnotic.

CLASSICAL MUSIC - Tchaikovsky - Swan Lake, The Nutcracker Suite and of course... Romeo and Juliet
   The following four albums are better suited for after dinner and intimate situations. They start off nice and slow and build up to powerful, and erotic, crescendos: · Rossini - The Thieving Magpie · Beethoven's Ninth - especially the finale · Dukas - The Sorcerer's Apprentice · And lets not forget... Ravel's "Bolero"

OLDIES BUT GOODIES - Moody Blues - Days of Future Passed · Pink Floyd - Dark Side of the Moon · Renaissance - Scherezade · Brian Ferry - Boys and Girls - I haven't met a woman yet who didn't like this album! Plus... Roxy Music with Brian Ferry - Avalon & Flesh and Blood both have memorable cuts.

NEWER MUSIC - George Michael - Older · Toni Braxton - First CD for sure, second CD has its moments · Trey Lorenz - Not bad at all!

For something really different: Hunters - Soundtrack from Discovery Channel TV Series. A very interesting recording that gives you the opportunity to set the mood for a "Jungle Theme" rendezvous - Perfect for an intimate evening after visiting the Wild Animal Park or Zoo.

Romantic Texas · 137

Unique Ideas for Romantic Gifts

by Michelle Garmon

Women love to receive flowers for any occasion. It is especially fun to have arrangements delivered to her workplace, certain to be the "talk of the office" and sure to be pleasing. Another way to send flowers is to leave a small bouquet or one single red rose on your sweetheart's car or front porch start her day off with a smile.

Photos always make a nice gift and can be very romantic, whether they are sophisticated, boudoir, black and white or colour portraits. Family portraits, mother or father and child, all make great anniversary presents. Favorite romantic songs, old movies or poetry books also make great sentimental selections.

Hobby related gardening books on roses (with a supplied rosebush) or reading material on other hobbies or interests also make excellent choices.

A different twist to "bouquet" gift giving is the balloon bouquet or the cookie bouquet. Both are fun and unusual. Wrap your gift and make it stand out in originality. Packages, stuffed animals, flowers, candy or just about anything can be wrapped inside a balloon with confetti, proving very unusual and a show stopper.

Gift certificates are always nice to receive and can be purchased for just about any product or service. Some great ideas include pedicures, manicures, facials, his or her massages, comedy clubs, clothing, dance lessons, etc. For him, certificates for golf rounds, one day cruises, sporting events, wine tasting, seminars, etc. Gift giving is always a pleasure and shows any special someone that you are thinking about them.

The Art of Buying Flowers

Yes, there is an art to buying flowers without spending a fortune for something you aren't sure is right for the occasion.

Lately, women and men alike not only seem to enjoy the spontaneity of flowers, but the fact that you know what is involved in putting together a nice arrangement without being ostentatious. Try something other than the basics, like carnations or roses. For instance, a strand or two of mini-orchids or Peruvian lily with a sprig of baby's breath and one or two fern leaves, make for a memorable and reasonably priced arrangement. And a sunflower will always brighten somebody's day.

Discuss with the florist that you would like something different for around $5.00 or $10.00 and you may be surprised at the selection available to you. Pick a couple of favorite flowers and then leave it up to the florist to make an enticing bouquet. Watch carefully as to how it is put together for future reference.

Despite what some might think about the stigma of buying flowers for guys, many men like flowers, too! Presented in a vase he can call his own, daisies, freshly blooming lilies or Protea are sure to delight.

Note: Be careful about buying roses on a warm or hot day if you plan on walking around a lot. Even though you can buy them with the end of the stems in small vials of water, they are a delicate and easily damaged flower that if bruised would disappoint your friend. Instead, select a more durable flower that can be enjoyed for a couple of days.

A nice touch to a special day, surprise your partner and you just might get the chance to steal that kiss you've been waiting for!

Weddings & Anniversaries

Depending on your budget or desires, weddings can be extravagant events or as simple as a delightful ceremony in a favorite park. Often times the simple and uncomplicated ceremonies outdoors are the best.

And of course things do go wrong at times (someone once told me to expect at least three things to happen during the ceremony), so make the most of the situation and savor the memories forever.

For an ideal small wedding, make arrangements for you and your guests to reserve an entire Bed and Breakfast for a weekend (of course, take the honeymoon suite for yourself). People will remember your special day for years to come!

Anniversaries are a special opportunity to do something nice for that person you love. It's your chance to let your partner know how happy you are, not only that you are together, but that you are *still* together. Anniversaries are a great occasion to put your creativity to work and plan a romantic outing for just the two of you. The date is already set, and special moments always seem more alive on this day. Going the extra mile will show your lover just how much you care (now if you could just remember the date!).

Weddings & Anniversaries Gift Giving

The following is a list of traditional and contemporary ideas for anniversary presents:

First	Paper	Clocks
Second	Cotton	China
Third	Leather	Leather
Fourth	Fruit/Flowers	Appliances
Fifth	Wood	Silverware
Sixth	Candy/Iron	Wood
Seventh	Wool/Copper	Desk Sets
Eighth	Bronze/Pottery	Linens/Lace
Ninth	Pottery/Willow	Crystal/Glass
Tenth	Tin/Aluminum	Diamond Jewelry
Eleventh	Steel	Fashion Jewelry
Twelfth	Silk/Linen	Pearls
Thirteenth	Lace	Textiles/Furs
Fourteenth	Ivory	Gold Jewelry
Fifteenth	Crystal	Watches
Twentieth	China	Platinum
Twenty-fifth	Silver	Silver
Thirtieth	Pearl	Diamond
Thirty-fifth	Coral	Jade
Fortieth	Ruby	Ruby
Forty-fifth	Sapphire	Sapphire
Fiftieth	Gold	Gold
Fifty-fifth	Emerald	Emerald
Sixtieth	Diamond	Diamond

SEXY THINGS TO DO:

♥ Take massage lessons together (*or buy the book "The Art of Sensual Massage"*), buy some fragrant massage oil, (*almond, is a favourite!*) light a bunch of candles, put on some mellow music and practice assorted techniques until you get it right. Be sure to have on hand soft cushy towels and a spray bottle with alcohol for an enjoyable, after massage wipe down.

♥ Nice touches after the massage: A mink glove rubdown highlighted by a string of pearls (available at any women's accessories shop) drawn along the curves of the body. A sensual experience to share with a loved one!

♥ Soak fresh strawberries in your glass of champagne and then share strawberry kisses.

♥ LADIES....Put on your favourite shade of BRIGHT lipstick and give the mirror in his bathroom or the drivers window on his car a BIG KISS!! Or, stuff one of his bed pillows into a lace teddy (you know, the one you wore the night before!!) attach a note that says "THINK OF ME!"

♥ Leave a long stemmed rose to be discovered... In the bottom of the bathtub - On a pillow - Tied to a toothbrush.

♥ Spray some cologne or perfume on your lover's pillow and put a sexy card or note underneath. Although, even without the note, the memory of the night before will be drifting through their dreams all night - guaranteed!

♥ Want to give someone a particularly memorable kiss? Add some steam to the atmosphere by outlining just your lovers lips with the very tip of your tongue, then plant a soft, sexy, heart-felt kiss on those ruby reds.

♥ Set up your living room in front of the fireplace like you were at the beach. Spread a blanket out, plants or palms, sprinkle glitter on them and the surrounding area and set out a picnic with champagne. A record of the ocean or even the Beach Boys for background music will do nicely. Strategically place stuffed birds or animals around the room can add some additional fun.

♥ CONSERVE WATER - Join your sweetie in the shower, but try a different twist to this romantic interlude. Put on a washable teddy (gals) sexy underwear (guys) and then step into the steam - guaranteed to fog up the bathroom mirror!

Index

Bed & Breakfast Inns

A Little Waltz & The Texas Two Step	82
Albion B&B	97
Angel Arbor B&B	111
Ant Street Inn	105
Austin's Wildflower Inn	54
Baker St. Inn	24
Blair House	62
Boat & Breakfast	132
Bonner Garden B&B	92
Briarfield At Round Top B&B	103
Brookhaven Manor	91
Captains Quarters	118
Carson House & Grill	21
Casa De Esperanza	58
Catalina Island Inn	131
Charles House	23
Charnwood Hill Inn	15
Chaska House	32
Cityview	52
Crystal River Inn	64
Durham House B&B	116
Fairview B&B	49
Far View	106
Finer Things	75
Fortuna Bay B&B	128
Governor's Inn	50
Gruene Country Homestead	72
Gruene Mansion	68
Hale House	25
Harrison B&B	34
Highlander B&B	112
Houston House	98
Karbach House	75
Kuebler – Waldrip Haus	71
Madame Dryers	121
Mariposa Ranch	108
Miss Molly's B&B	38
Moonlight Bay	126
Munzesheimer Manor	16
Nobel Inns	88
Nueces Canyon	107
O' Casey's	90
Oxford House	45
Patrician	114
Pearl St. Inn	39
Lily House	41
Hummingbird Lodge	42
Prince Solms Inn	73
Roses And The River	125
Southwind	63
The Cabin On The Lake	94
The Settlement House	101
Thee Hubble House	18
Trails End	57
Watkins Hill	80
Whispering Pines	28

Hotels

Bahia Mar Hotel	130
Bayfront Port Royal	127
Best Western	26
Hotel Galvez	123
Hyatt Hill Country Resort	87
La Mansion	85
Lancaster Hotel	115
Ramada Hotel	127
Red Roof Inn	92
Renaissance Austin Hotel	55
St. Anthony Hotel	86
Tremont House	122
Worthington Hotel	37

Restaurant Reviews

Bistro Lancaster	115
Carmellos	51
Carson House & Grill	21
Catfish Plantation Restaurant	30
Dove's Nest Restaurant	30
Favourite Austin Restaurants	53
Grey Moss Inn	87
Hilltop Cafe	78
Hudson On The Bend	56
Las Canaris	85
Mesa	113
Restaurant At Gruene Mansion	69
Round Top Cafe	100
Scampi's	130
The Plateau	78
The Riverside Bayou	85
Vargo's	113
Victoria Black Swan	86

Texas Towns

Austin	48	Riverwalk	84
Brazoria	124	Texas Eagle Train Line	14
Brenham	104	The Texas Hill Country	60
Caddo Lake	27	Things To Do In Gonzales	98
Corpus Christi	127	Wildflower Trails	20
Fort Worth	36	**Lone Star Rendezvous**	
Fredericksburg	78	Brenham	104
Galveston Island	119	Galveston	122
Glen Rose	40	New Braunfels	70
Gonzales	96	The Hill Country	61
Granbury3	9	**Proffessional Services**	
Gruene	67	A Poem Into A Song	94
Houston	110	Bed And Breakfast Reservation Center	114
Jefferson	22	Creative Chocolates	86
Kemah	119	Ferrentino Therapeutic Massage	129
Kerrville	77	Gästehaus Schmidt	
Lockhart	96	~ B&B Reservation Service	79
Mineola	13	Historical Accommodations Of Texas	9
New Braunfels	70	**Romantic Information**	
Padre Island National Seashore	129	A Secret Formula Of Love	16
Palacios	124	About The Author	143
Pittsburg	20	Bed & Breakfast Inns	8
Port Aransas/Mustang Island	129	Buying The Right Rose	
Round Top	100	For The Right Occasion	46
San Antonio	84	Children & Romantic Getaways	7
San Marcos	65	First Dates & Inexpensive Dating Tips	89
South Padre Island	129	Getting Away From The Big City	12
Stephanville	44	Index	141
Tyler	13	Is It Really Romantic	6
Waxahachie	30	Packing A Picnic Basket	135
Wimberly	60	Rainy Days And Sundays	31
Winsborro	14	Romantic Dining	8
Neat Things To Do		Romantic Dinners At Home	134
Antiquing	12	Romantic Movies	136
Caddo Lake Steamboat Co.	27	Romantic Music	137
Driving In Texas	93	Romantic Texas	10
Enchanted Rock State Natural Area	82	Sexy Things To Do	140
In Search Of The Antiquelope	12	Stargazing	15
King Williams District	87	Texas Map	4
Lake O' The Pines	24	Texas Sunsets	94
Lake Travis	55	The Art Of Buying Flowers	139
Majestic Theater	84	The Art Of Dating	40
Monte Vista	89	The Art Of Romance	6
Moonlight Drive	79	The Impeccable Picnic	135
Mystique Tours	27	The Romantic Highway	4
North Central Texas		Unique Ideas For Gifts	138
Romantic Drives	43 & 44	Wedding Anniversary Gift Giving	139
North East Texas Driving Excursion	26	Weddings & Anniversaries	138
Padre Island National Seashore	129		

About the Author

Ken Christensen, author, artist and entrepreneur was born in a log cabin he helped his father build. Trudging through rain, sleet and snow to come home with C average grades, he relentlessly pursued his education in the School of Hard Knocks and the College of Life, while studying the philosophies of Howard, Howard and Fine. At the age of 17, he took on a summer job as a laborer for a bricklayer and decided, then and there, that he was going to be an artist!

15+ years in the printing industry has given him the knowledge and opportunity to fulfill his dream of getting out of the printing industry! Luck prevailed and he now publishes and produces the Romantic America book series which, delightfully enough, people seem to like!

The Cabin On The Lake

This cozy and private cabin has a scenic view of a peaceful lake in Linden, Texas (north of Jefferson). In late 1997, this will become a private retreat for those seeking the ultimate in total seclusion. Privacy is yours to savour in this little slice of heaven! If a Romantic Rendezvous is on your mind, a path leads into the woods and offers many unforgettable picnic spots. At night the stars shine brightly above and twinkle lights frame the house. Bring your favourite romantic tapes, fixin's for a candlelight dinner and unforgettable memories are sure to be yours. If it rains, don't worry! This is the ideal place to snuggle in bed all day while savouring the sound of rain on the tin roof. For more information, call

1.800.442.4815

Sunshine Thoughts For The Morning After

Breakfast in bed is one of the most exciting and wonderful sensations following a night of intimacy. A quick shower before dining followed by a long one together afterwards is always special. A breakfast with fresh juice, muffins, eggs, coffee and champagne is always appreciated. Served on a tray with china, nice silverware, cloth napkins and a flower in a vase are very special touches. A great way to start a lazy day or to use as an excuse to stay in bed all day enjoying each others company.

And remember...

Use Your Imagination!

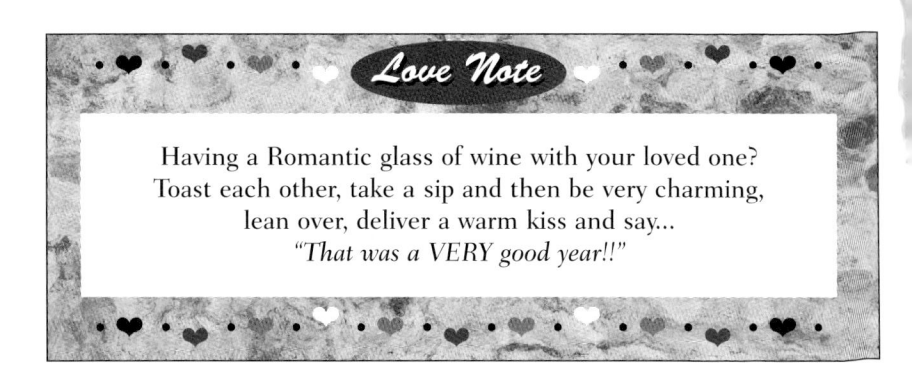

Love Note

Having a Romantic glass of wine with your loved one? Toast each other, take a sip and then be very charming, lean over, deliver a warm kiss and say...
"That was a VERY good year!!"